NVQ Level 2

Heinemann

Student Handbook

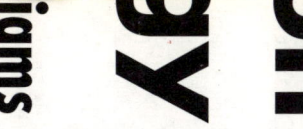

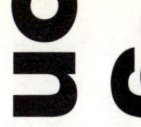

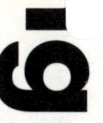

Heinemann Educational Publishers, Halley Court, Jordan Hill, Oxford OX2 8EJ
A division of Reed Educational & Professional Publishing Ltd

Heinemann is a registered trademark of Reed Educational & Professional Publishing Limited

OXFORD MELBOURNE AUCKLAND JOHANNESBURG BLANTYRE GABORONE
IBADAN PORTSMOUTH NH (USA) CHICAGO

First published 2002
2006 2005 2004 2003 2002
10 9 8 7 6 5 4 3 2 1

A catalogue record for this book is available from the British Library on request.

ISBN 0 435 45162 6

Typeset and illustrated by Techype, Abingdon, Oxon

Printed and bound in Great Britain by Biddles Ltd, Guildford

Tel: 01865 888058 www.heinemann.co.uk

Contents

Introduction		1
About the NVQ		1
Working with data		3
The legislation		8

MANDATORY UNITS

Unit 206	Ensure Your Own Actions Reduce Risks to Health and Safety	15
Unit 301	Select and Enable Information Technology for Use	30
Unit 302	Maintain the Software Environment	46
Unit 303	Develop and Maintain the Effectiveness of the Information Technology Working Environment	58
Unit 308	Develop Your Own Effectiveness and Professionalism	66

OPTIONAL UNITS

Unit 305	Design and Produce Documents Using Word Processing Software	73
Unit 306	Design and Produce Spreadsheets	91
Unit 311	Design and Use Databases	108
Unit 312	Design and Produce Documents Using Graphics	123
Unit 326	Design and Produce Presentations Using Information Technology	133
Unit 327	Control the Use of Electronic Communication	143

Case study: Autoware	157
Appendix: Jobs in ICT	163
NVQ glossary	184
IT glossary	186
Index	189

Acknowledgements

The author and publisher would like to thank the following organisations for permission to reproduce copyright material:

Imagebank/Peter Pacifica
Microsoft Corporation
Telegraph Colour Library/Jean Louis Batt

Introduction

About the NVQ

What is it?

An NVQ (National Vocational Qualification) is a specification that has been set by a national training organisation to define the work-based standards. The organisation for IT is the Information Technology National Training Organisation (ITNTO).

An NVQ consists of a number of units. A unit is a complete section of knowledge and skills. Each unit is broken down into a number of elements which are described by a set of performance criteria. These spell out the things you have to do and the skills and knowledge you need to demonstrate.

You are assessed against these standards and are required to demonstrate your competence for all the performance criteria and across a specified range (the scope and the variety) of activities.

The national framework classifies the level of achievement and competence at Level 3 as:

> "*Competence, which involves the application of knowledge in a broad range of varied work activities performed in a wide variety of contexts, most of which are complex and non-routine. There is considerable responsibility and autonomy and control or guidance of others is often required.*"

Further to this, the ITNTO have defined the standard for using IT as:

> "*Being consistently effective entering and manipulating data from undefined requirements to create a variety of complex documents using multiple applications, to appropriate destinations. Advise and assist others to resolve their IT problems within own area of expertise.*"

You will need to be carrying out a wide range of IT-related tasks, operating with considerable autonomy and which is likely to include responsibility for computer systems and the staff operating them. This work will need to include the design and implementation of operating procedures and providing staff with the training necessary to be able to use the systems effectively.

How is it assessed?

This qualification is about demonstrating your skills and knowledge in the workplace. To do this you need to collect evidence of your competence to do the work to the agreed standard. This evidence needs to be put together into a portfolio for assessment.

There are two main types of evidence: performance and supplementary.

Performance evidence results from doing the job and will consist of:

- end products – eg plans, hard copy, disk files, etc.
- observation of activities – your assessor will need to watch you carrying out some of the tasks that you need to include in your portfolio and record these observations.

Supplementary evidence may include:

- questions and answers (written and oral) – your assessor may ask you questions or provide you with a worksheet
- endorsed witness statements by yourself, supervisors or colleagues – these confirm that you have carried out an activity to the required standards and may be necessary where there is no end product
- previous certificates of competence, eg IT key skills Level 3 certificates.

As this is a vocational qualification, the primary sources of evidence of competence should be from performance evidence, ie real work that you have carried out. For some elements, it is also possible for assessment to take place in a realistic working environment – this is one which reflects the expectations of industry and commerce by efficiently and effectively using currently acceptable information technology systems.

What you need to do

You need to collect this evidence over a period of time, usually of at least six months, and present it in a portfolio. This portfolio will need to include the recording systems required by the awarding body. For each item of evidence you will need to show:

- which units, elements and performance criteria it is evidence towards
- who has assessed it
- when, where and under what conditions it was carried out.

You will need to compile an index and be able to cross-reference your documents.

The structure of the NVQ

To complete this NVQ, you are required to meet all the requirements of the five mandatory units and at least three of the six optional units, making eight units in total.

The mandatory units are primarily concerned with:

- best practice when working in an IT environment, including health and safety
- developing and improving your own professionalism and effectiveness in IT.

The optional units are concerned with:

- effective use of individual applications of IT.

Much of the evidence for the mandatory evidence can be provided by carrying out activities for the optional units you have chosen. For example, as you are producing word processing documents (Unit 305) you will also be carrying out tasks that are to be assessed in Unit 301 (Select and Enable Information Technology for Use) and Element 303.1 (Plan and organise the effective use of information technology).

While this means that the evidence for one unit is also evidence for other units and can therefore reduce the overall volume of evidence to be collected, it can also make the recording, tracking and presentation of your completed work more complex. This makes the inclusion of an index and a good cross-referencing system all the more important.

Much of the qualification is concerned with effective and appropriate application and supervision of the technology. There is therefore considerable emphasis on the knowledge and skills of the specific software necessary to carry out the work. However, it is essential that you have a good understanding of all aspects of working with data and information. It is also important that you are able to demonstrate a good level of knowledge and awareness of the relevant legislation, especially with regard to data protection, computer misuse, software copyright and health and safety.

Working with data

A computer system can be described as input, processing and output. Data is input to the system; it is processed and information is output. Data is

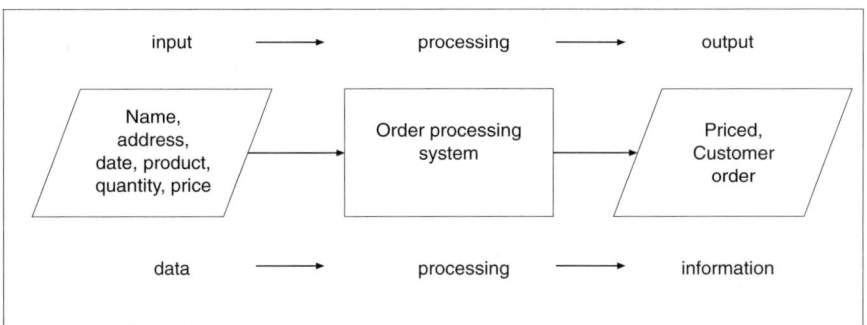

Figure 1 *Working with data*

the raw facts, information is data that has been processed and now has meaning.

The data, and resulting information, is often referred to as the life-blood of the organisation. Without data, in an accurate and secure form, the viability and future of the organisation may be threatened.

As an autonomous user with responsibilities for at least part of a system and/or staff working with the system, you need to have a good understanding of the importance of the data.

There are two key areas that you will need to consider:

- integrity
- security.

Data integrity

Integrity of data refers to the correctness of the data throughout its life in the system. As an expert user, you must ensure that all the work you do, and those you are responsible for, ensures the integrity of the data. You will need to ensure that you set up systems and procedures to ensure the integrity of data at input, during processing and at output.

At point of input

Capture of appropriate data:

- You should collect and store the data in the best way so that it will not need processing just to keep it current. (For example, date of birth rather than age, as the latter becomes incorrect as time goes by.)

Verification of data:

- This involves checks to make sure that the data is entered accurately. (For example, the data is entered twice into the computer by different people, the two versions are compared by the computer and any data with differences is rejected for checking and re-input.)
- Check digits are extra digits, usually in an account number, which are based on the numbers in the account number and their sequence. If any number is entered incorrectly, or the numbers are entered in the wrong order, then the check digit will indicate that this is not a valid account number. (For example, in an invoicing system, the customer account number has an additional digit which ensures that if any one digit of the code is entered incorrectly then it should be identified as an error *before* the invoice is raised for the wrong customer. This doesn't mean that the invoice is correct but it does mean that it will be sent to the right customer.)
- On-screen checking, that is visual checking (proof reading). (For example, when the customer account number is entered, the name and

address are displayed on the screen for the operator to check before continuing with the rest of the input.)

Validation of data:

- This is to make sure that it is an allowed value or response. (For example, the payroll system may be set up to accept only a range of values as no one has a salary above or below a limit, or to make sure that only the correct names of departments can be entered, they are selected from a 'pick list'.)
- Batch totals, for example, are particularly important when handling numeric, mainly financial, data. (For example, the total value of a set of invoices is calculated manually and entered at the start of the input process. As each invoice is input, the computer system keeps a running total of all of the invoices. When the complete set (batch) has been input, the computer system compares the input total with the calculated total and will only accept the batch if the totals match.)

Case Study Activity

Information about the company Autoware has been included in the form of a case study on pp. 157–62. It describes the nature and structure of the organisation and will provide you with a context in which to carry out this task. It is therefore essential that you read this before you attempt this activity.

When a licence for software is purchased by a new customer, the data items need to be input into the system. This will include details about the customer, the number of users, the type of licence, the costs and the maintenance agreement attached to it.

Suggest examples of procedures to ensure the integrity of the data using:

- appropriate data

- verification of data

- validation of data.

During processing

Testing:

- When systems are developed, there must be thorough testing of each part of the system and also full systems testing to make sure that all the parts work together correctly. One of the reasons that computer systems produce errors is that, at the testing stage, only sensible data is used. Unfortunately, there are many occasions when a user will input erroneous data.

- It is essential that a full testing strategy is used to ensure the integrity of the system. A test plan should be drawn up for every activity (input, process and output) in the system, identifying the data and the expected results. This should include tests using *expected* data (the usual data), *extreme* data (upper and lower limits that can be accepted) and *invalid* data (all kinds of possible responses including absolute rubbish).

Authorised access (see security, p. 51).

Processing controls:

- **Control totals** are produced by the system at various stages of a process and should be checked manually as well as by the system to identify any errors or corruption of data. (For example, in a cheque printing system, during the first stage of the process which involves identifying those suppliers for whom cheques are to be printed, the total value of all cheques will be calculated together with the total number of cheques. This control information will be printed and also passed on to the next stage of the process. As the cheques are printed, a running total will be made of the values together with a count of how many cheques exist. These second process control totals will be compared by the computer system at the end of the process but should also be printed for a manual check.)

- **Check sums** are similar to check digits and are used to ensure that the numbers and sequence of numbers are not corrupted as the data is passed from one process or system to another. (For example, all the retail outlets of a chain store send their sales data through a communications link to the head office every evening after close of business. A mathematical formula is applied to this numeric data and from this an additional item of data (the *check value*) is derived. When the data is sent to the central computer system this additional item is also sent. When the data is received the same formula is applied and the two check values are compared to make sure they are the same. If they are not, the receiving computer can send a message requesting that the data is sent again as there is apparently an error.)

Backup and recovery procedures (see p. 51).

At output

- Testing: when an output is designed, it must be tested and checked to make sure that the information is correct; this should be included as part of the test plan for processing (see above).
- Formatting: integrity of data can be lost at output if the way the information is displayed is incorrect. It is possible, for example, within a database report to fail to format the data and as a result not all of it is displayed.

Data security

Adequate controls are needed throughout a system to ensure that there is only authorised access to the data. This can be achieved through:

- Passwords
  These can be used for access to a system, access to an application and access to a set of data. For example, in your place of work your password will probably give you access to the main set of programs, such as word processing and spreadsheet packages, but only if you work in the finance department can you also access the accounts system, and only if you are responsible for managing the department can you also access the budget data. It is essential that passwords are changed regularly. For example, in most organisations the system will automatically prompt you after a set number of days.

- Communication controls
  These are necessary to ensure that only authorised people can connect to the system through an external link. For example, the system of 'dial-back' is used in many organisations. When a user connects to the computer through an external link, the system will know from the user's log in details who he or she is and will have details of the authorised user's telephone number. The link is immediately disconnected and the computer 'dials back' to the external system.

- Physical controls
  Computer equipment, and therefore access to the information, may need to be located in a secure environment. Careful consideration needs to be given to the positioning of equipment, particularly where computers are in areas with unrestricted access, and users need to follow procedures about exiting from the systems so that information is not left displayed on the screen.

Case Study Activity

Using the Autoware Case Study on pp. 157–62.

The organisation will need to have a range of controls to ensure the security of its systems. Draw up a list of suggestions to be considered to include:

- passwords
- communication controls
- physical controls.

The legislation

The use of computers in all areas of work and leisure is growing rapidly. As a computer user, you need to know about the various aspects of legislation relating to working with computers. The main areas that you need to be particularly aware of are data protection, copyright issues and computer misuse. You also need to know about the health and safety requirements which are covered in detail in Unit 206.

Data Protection Act

What is meant by data protection and why is it necessary? More and more information about people is being stored on computers and more and more people have easier access to it.

- Worldwide communication systems are becoming more powerful by the day. It is now possible for data held almost anywhere in the world to be accessed rapidly in most other parts of the world.
- The speed and processing power of computers means that facts and figures about individuals are more likely to be analysed and brought together.
- The proliferation of computers in both businesses and the home means that almost anyone has access to this technology. The costs of online access are reducing rapidly, so this expansion will undoubtedly continue.

There are many advantages to this widespread computerised data access, but it brings with it the need to ensure that the data, and the individuals concerned, are protected. How many organisations do you think hold data about you in an electronic form?

Figure 2 shows a table of likely computerised record holders for most people in the UK today. The list is by no means complete, but is intended to highlight the extent of electronic collection and storage of personal data. Most of the time we are not made aware that this information is going to be held as a permanent record and we rarely think twice about supplying the details. Although data users are required to advise you that this information will be held, and to give you the opportunity to request that they do not make it available elsewhere, it is often in such small print that you don't notice it.

It is extremely important that all personnel in the organisation who have any role with data covered by the Act are fully aware of what is involved. Whenever you are responsible for the design and development of an IT solution, you will need to take into consideration the requirements of the legislation. You will also need to make sure that all the staff for whom you have any responsibility are aware of the requirements and that they operate within these.

Organisation	Type of data	Tick the ones that apply to you
Health Authority	Personal details including name of doctor	
Doctor	Medical history	
Local Authority	Residential and possibly employment and benefit details	
Bank	Credit rating and history; some employment details	
Employer	Employment history; some medical records	
DVLC Swansea	Car and driving licence details	
PNC	Car details	
Inland Revenue	Tax and employment history	
Education Authority	Education and some family details	
Insurance companies	Motor – motoring offences, driving details and history Life – health, employment, family details Home – home security, value of possessions	
Credit card and hire purchase companies	Credit rating, income, expenditure, lifestyle	
Societies and organisations e.g. AA, RAC, Reader's Digest etc.	Limited but tend to have lifestyle details	
Internet service provider (ISP)	Basic personal details plus details of Internet usage and payment history	
Telephone providers – mobile and land line	Basic personal details plus details of telephone usage and payment history	
Large retail outlets where you have used a credit card	Basic personal details plus details of purchasing history	

Figure 2 *Computerised record holders in the UK*

What is the legislation?

The legislation that needs to be considered comes from both (a) that which relates specifically to the UK and is usually made by the passing of an Act of Parliament; and (b) the requirements of the European Union, which are usually set down as directives to which all member countries must then conform. The current British legislation is contained within the 1998 **Data**

Protection Act which replaces the 1984 Act. The 1984 Act was concerned with "Personal Data", information about living, identifiable individuals, which is "automatically processed". The 1998 Act sets rules for processing personal information and applies to organised paper records as well as those held on computer.

It is based upon eight guiding principles:
- Data must be processed lawfully and fairly – this includes the requirement that this data has also been obtained fairly and lawfully and that the data subject has been notified of the intention to process this data.
- Data must be held only for specified purposes – these have to be identified at registration.
- Data must be adequate, relevant and not excessive – the amount of data held should be the minimum necessary to meet the specified purposes.
- Data must be accurate and kept up to date.
- Data must not be held for longer than is necessary.
- Data subjects should be able to access their data and, where appropriate, have it corrected or deleted.
- Security systems must exist to ensure that unauthorised users cannot access, process, alter, destroy or disclose data.
- Data must not be transferred to a country outside the European Economic Area, unless that country has a similar level of protection for the rights of data subjects.

How does it work?
The main operational aspects of this Act are the requirements on all data controllers (the person within an organisation who determines how and why data is to be processed) to:
- notify the details of the types of data they hold and for what purposes
- ensure that their systems have adequate controls to maintain the integrity of the data
- ensure that they have adequate security on their systems to safeguard against unauthorised access
- set up procedures to enable the data subject access to their data and to have corrected any inaccuracies, unnecessary records or misuse.

There is no requirement to notify manual records covered by the Data Protection Act, although they can be notified voluntarily.

The process of notification can be carried out using either the Internet, completing an online form or by telephone when a draft notification form is completed based on the information provided during the conversation which is then sent for confirmation.

The Data Protection Register, which contains the details supplied by the data controllers, is a public document maintained by the Data Protection Commissioner. A copy should be available in major public libraries and you can carry out a search on the Data Protection website.

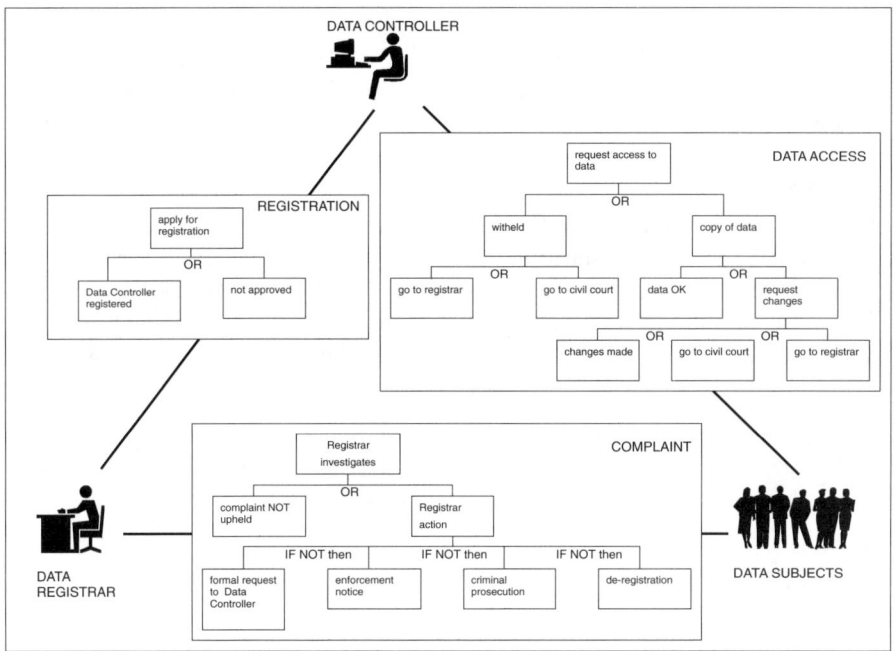

Figure 3 *How the Data Protection Act 1998 operates*

Case Study Activity

Using the Autoware Case Study on pp. 157–62.

Assuming that some of the data about customer personnel that will be held in the Autoware system are covered by the Data Protection Act, draw up a set of instructions for the staff with access to the data to ensure that all uses of the data comply with the legislation.

Copyright

Copyright is about the ownership of rights in printed and recorded materials and software. It restricts what you are allowed to copy, how many times and for what purposes. The contents of this book are covered by copyright law. The author and publisher had to make sure that the words and images did not 'belong' to anyone else. The copyright of this book belongs to the author. If you wish to use something that belongs to someone else, you must seek permission, acknowledge their copyright and, usually, pay to be allowed to use it. If you don't, it is the same as stealing.

There are two different areas of concern regarding copyright and IT. One relates to software and the conditions under which you are permitted to use it and the other is about the use of data, images and text which are held in digital form.

Once again, you will need to ensure that not only do you comply with copyright but that you also provide support and training to staff for whom you are responsible.

Software

Software is very costly to produce and very easy to copy. When you acquire an item of software you do not usually own the software – what you have purchased is a licence to use it. There are many different types of licences and it is always important to read the small print to make sure you are aware of what you can and cannot do. The licence could be any one of the following:

- Single user licence

  You may use this software on one computer only – the licence is usually for the user, who may transfer the software from one machine to another as long as it can be used on only one machine at any time.

- Multi-user licence

  You may have up to an agreed number of users with access to this software – this may be by installation on a set number of computers, or it could be for specified numbers with network access.

  This can usually be monitored by the network software keeping count of the number of users at any one time, thereby ensuring that the licence level is not exceeded.

- Site licence

  You may be licensed to use the software for all the users on a site – some software providers consider a site to mean a physical location, whilst others can interpret it more loosely and it could mean a whole organisation.

- Machine licence

  Sometimes the software licence is attached to a particular computer rather than the user – in this instance you cannot transfer the software to a different computer without the permission of the copyright holder.

- Server licence

  On a network, the licence may be restricted, like a machine licence, to a particular network server.

- Network licence

  In a network environment you may have a licence for software to be used across the whole network – again there are a number of different ways the term 'network' is interpreted. Most network systems software will be licensed under a network licence.

It is illegal to copy and use software in a way that has not been licensed. It is extremely unlikely that anyone working in an IT department would ask you to do this. It is, however, possible that someone who doesn't understand copyright could ask you; for example, a person who has some software on a computer at home and would like to use it at work. If this happens, you should politely explain the law and consult your supervisor.

Some software is provided on a different basis, such as shareware and freeware. This is often software that has not been developed by a commercial organisation and therefore there is not the same concern about loss of income through unauthorised copying.

Shareware software is usually freely distributed in an unsupported form. It will usually come with details of how you can pay a nominal charge which will entitle you to patches (corrections), add-ons (enhanced features) and updates.

Freeware is software for which there is no charge, and can be freely distributed and used. This sort of software is not usually a full-feature application but often consists of a number of utilities and useful routines. This may be distributed through CD-ROMs attached to magazines, etc., or could be available on the Internet.

Data, images and text

In recent years the development of technologies that enable data, images and text to be readily captured and held in digital form has considerably increased concern about copyright. All the aspects of copyright in the print world now also apply in the digital world, but are more complex and potentially more difficult to control.

Scanners and software which not only capture images and store them electronically but also have the capability to convert scanned text pages into text characters that can then be manipulated through word processors, etc. are now very cheaply and readily available. Access to the Internet, and the ability to freely down-load information in any form, provides a major potential source of information. This means that large quantities of words can be rapidly stored, altered and transmitted across networks. It also means that in the course of your everyday work, it would be easy to reproduce text and images belonging to someone else, without considering the fact that you are breaching copyright regulations.

Computer misuse

A whole range of activities can be considered under the term misuse. The Computer Misuse Act 1995 identified three types of crime.

Breaking in

The act of breaking into a computer system (hacking) is in itself a crime. It is also the first stage of doing damage to the system. Employees' carelessness with passwords is a common cause of unauthorised access. Also, particularly in a system where there are a great many users and passwords, hackers can find out passwords by trial and error. Too many people choose 'obvious' character combinations for their passwords, such as their date of birth, the name of a friend or member of the family. To a skilled and determined hacker these are their first choices when attempting a break in.

Breaking in with further criminal intent

If someone hacks into a system for reasons other than just to do it, then he or she has committed a further crime. With the increasing use of computers for design purposes, many product plans may be vulnerable to theft through unauthorised access by competitors. Valuable customer details and company 'secrets' can be stolen and sold to competitors for profit.

Alteration of data and programs

Once inside the computer system the hacker, or other unauthorised user, may gain access to sensitive data. Employees and others from outside the organisation may alter data for their own benefit. Changes may be made to an employee's payroll data so that he or she is 'overpaid'; accounts receivable entries may be wiped out so that a customer is not charged for goods received; or accounts and charges in an accounts payable system may be set up so that customers are charged (and possibly pay) for goods or services they never receive. Finally there is the possibility of wilful destruction of an entire database; this can be guarded against by the operation of regular and comprehensive backup procedures.

Sometimes a minor change to a program can enable someone to profit fraudulently. There have been a number of examples where employees have transferred the 'rounded down' fractions of amounts of money to their own or fictitious accounts and have succeeded, over several years, in committing significant thefts.

Theft of computer time

Many people use their access to their employer's computers to carry out their own activities. It is not at all uncommon for employees to word process the occasional personal letter, or to prepare their CVs to help them apply for new jobs. These activities are rarely considered to be a major problem although they are still a misuse of the computer system. However, there are many instances of employees using their employers' computer system to carry out activities for which they are being paid by others. In many organisations this would be treated as a disciplinary offence for which you could be sacked.

The Regulation of Investigatory Powers (RIP) Act

This Act is an update to the law on interception of communications and takes into account the development of new technologies and particularly the Internet. It gives e-mails the same standing as telephone calls and letters allowing the interception of e-mail by government. Corporations can monitor employees' online behaviour as long as they have stated their plans to do so. The Data Protection Commissioner has issued a code of practice covering the use of personal data in employment which recognises the right of employers to monitor e-mails and Internet use. However, this indicates that there must be a clear business need and the level of monitoring must not be excessive.

MANDATORY UNITS

Unit 206 Ensure Your Own Actions Reduce Risks to Health and Safety

This unit contains two elements:

206.1 Identify the hazards and evaluate the risks in your workplace
206.2 Reduce the risks to health and safety in your workplace.

You need to demonstrate that your actions do not create health and safety risks and that you do not ignore significant risks and potential hazards in your workplace. You will also need to demonstrate that you take appropriate and sensible actions to put things right.

To meet the requirements of this unit, you should have a good understanding of where responsibility lies for health and safety within your organisation. You should know about the legislation that relates to the workplace and particularly to working in an information technology environment. You will also need to be able to identify risks arising from hazards and know what you can deal with safely and what should be reported to a 'responsible person'.

You will need to ensure that not only do you operate in a safe manner, but you will also need to provide sufficient information and training to ensure that all staff for whom you are responsible are able to meet these requirements.

There are two main aspects to consider:

- general health and safety; and

- working in an information technology environment.

General health and safety

The main legislation is the Health and Safety at Work Act 1974. This legislation places the responsibility for health and safety in the workplace with both the employer and the employee.

Employers must:

- ensure that the workplace is safe and without risk to the health of their employees
- ensure that the workplace is clean and control the levels of dust, fumes and noise
- ensure that both plant and machinery are safe to work with, and that safe work practices are set and followed
- provide employees with all necessary information, instruction, training and supervision for health and safety
- put in place and implement a health and safety policy
- provide any protective clothing and equipment that is specifically required by health and safety legislation
- report injuries, diseases and dangerous incidents to the appropriate enforcing authority
- provide adequate first aid facilities and training
- take adequate precautions to prevent fire and provide appropriate means of fire fighting
- provide adequate means of escape
- maintain a workroom temperature of at least 16°C after the first hour of work where employees do most of their work sitting down
- provide, maintain and keep clean washing and toilet facilities
- ensure that employees do not have to lift, carry or move any load so heavy that it is likely to injure them
- ensure that objects and substances are stored and used safely.

The employee must:

- comply with the organisation's routine health and safety procedures
- take appropriate action if a hazardous or potentially hazardous situation arises
- ensure that his or her own work area is tidy and free from hazards.

Hazards in the working environment

Many aspects of the working environment present a hazard or potential hazard. Hazards are those aspects of the environment, the equipment and working practices which are unsafe. A potential hazard is often something less obvious.

When does a potential hazard become a hazard? It is all too easy, but could result from:

- carelessness or lack of attention
- lack of foresight
- rushing tasks or taking short-cuts

- a coincidence of circumstances or
- a change in circumstances.

Almost all hazards are avoidable if thought about beforehand.

Most workplaces have potential hazards which can result in accidents, such as:

- the shiny floor turns into a skating rink when a cup of coffee is spilt on it
- the open window gets caught by a sudden strong gust of wind, and slams shut and shatters
- the fizzy drink beside the computer gets knocked over and not only damages the keyboard but could cause an electrical hazard
- the filing cabinet drawer next to your desk is left open where someone could walk into it
- the computer is moved to another part of the room creating a lot of stress on the cables as they only just reach
- particles of toner are being continually released into the air from the laser printer in the main working area
- passage ways are obstructed
- cables are frayed or damaged
- plugs are unearthed.

What should you do about a hazard? If it is within your control – deal with it:

- Make sure that when boxes of stationery are delivered they are put away safely.
- Move the waste bin from the passageway before someone trips up.
- Explain the dangers of using a swivel chair to stand on.

As you may have responsibility for the working environment, and possibly staff, you should encourage people to report potential hazards before an accident happens. If it isn't within your control to rectify it, then you should report it to someone who can deal with it. You should make sure that everyone concerned is aware of reporting procedures and these should be straightforward and not be too time consuming, or people will not bother. Training and the use of clear, simple signs can often assist in raising awareness.

Figure 4 shows a typical modern office. However, it is not an entirely safe environment. Identify the risks that exist within the environment and how you would deal with each one. This should include the nature of the problem, the person or persons responsible, the recommended remedy and any further action that could be taken to ensure that this type of problem does not arise again. Include this information and a copy of the picture in your evidence folder.

Figure 4 *Identify the hazards in this working environment*

Emergencies

Accidents

Employers are required to take all reasonable steps to make sure that the workplace is a safe environment. Any accidents that do occur must be reported and recorded. This record has to be kept for 30 years. The circumstances of the accident must be investigated and, if it is serious, may have to be reported to the HSE (Health & Safety Executive).

First aid

Under the Health and Safety (First Aid) Regulations organisations are required to provide first aid facilities including qualified first aiders, first aid boxes and sometimes a first aid room. The level of provision is determined on the basis of the size of the organisation and how hazardous the environment is deemed to be. An office is potentially far less hazardous than a building site, for example. First aid boxes are not allowed to contain drugs nor can first aiders give out any medication – they could leave themselves open to legal action if someone had an adverse reaction to a drug he or she had been given.

Illness

If you are ill at home, you will normally be required to notify your supervisor, line manager or tutor that you are unable to come to work. You would then possibly arrange to see your doctor. However, there are times when you or a colleague becomes unwell whilst at work. In some instances, it may be necessary for a person who is unwell to go home. The person's supervisor should be notified, and assistance may be needed to get home.

In situations where an emergency arises, and you do not know the correct thing to do, make sure that you call a first aider immediately and don't try to deal with something outside your own scope. This can often make things much worse.

Many organisations will welcome requests by staff to become first aiders and will provide the necessary training. The expertise and knowledge that you get on a first aid course are extremely valuable to you not just at work, so consider finding out about it.

Fire

Employers can take a number of precautions against fire. For example, they can:

*   install fire doors
*   install fire extinguishers
*   install smoke detectors and sprinkler systems
*   restrict or ban smoking
*   arrange regular fire inspections with the fire brigade.

For the purposes of fire-fighting, fires are grouped into a number of different types (see Figure 5). A range of different fire extinguishers are available to cater for all these categories (see Figure 6).

Class of fire	Substance burning
A	paper, wood, fabric
B	liquids, fat, paint, spirits, oil
C	gases such as oxygen
D	metals such as magnesium
Electrical	

Figure 5 *Types of fires*

Colour	Contents	Class of fire
Red	water	A
Green	Halon, BCF	A, B, C, electrical
Cream	foam	A, B, C
Chrome	gas	A, B, C, electrical
Black	CO_2	B, C, electrical
Blue	powder	D

Figure 6 *Types of fire extinguishers*

N.B. All new portable extinguishers are coloured red, with a zone/panel of colour which indicates the contents.

Evacuation

There are a number of circumstances, in addition to fire, when it may be necessary to evacuate the building. These include:

- bomb threats
- severe flooding
- gas leaks.

The organisation where you work should have regular fire/evacuation drills and the alarms should be tested frequently to ensure that they all work.

CHECK IT YOURSELF

You may have responsibility for a number of staff within your organisation and will therefore be responsible for ensuring that they have the necessary information and training to work safely.

Investigate the health and safety of your working environment using the checklist on p. 27. Now use this information to prepare a training programme to ensure full awareness of safety in the workplace.

Working in an information technology environment

There are still many uncertainties about many aspects of a modern, technology-based working environment. Even now, not a great deal of information is available about the long-term effects of working in this kind of environment. Many people are understandably anxious about the possible effects, and in the past few years there has been a tightening up of the regulations and legal obligations of employers. The main legislation that relates to employer's obligations is primarily concerned with the use of display screen equipment (VDUs).

Health and Safety (Display Screen Equipment) Regulations 1992

The display screen equipment directives and regulations contain very specific requirements of the employer in relation to employees working with display screen equipment. You should be aware that these regulations apply only to employees. However, they are based upon good, safe working practice and ideally should exist in *all* computer areas, at home, work or college.

Regulation 1 – the user

The regulations define a user as an employee whether he or she is required to work at:

- a workstation on the employer's premises
- a workstation at home, or
- a workstation on another employer's premises.

The following factors are helpful in deciding if an employee is a user to which these regulations apply:

- The person relies on the use of display screen equipment to do the job.
- The person has no choice as to whether to use the equipment.
- Specific skills or training in the use of the equipment are necessary to do the job.
- The job can be carried out only through the use of the equipment for continuous spells of an hour or more at a time on a regular basis, probably daily.
- The job requires the fast transfer of information between the user and screen.
- The job demands high levels of attention and concentration by the user.

(**NOTE:** the definition of equipment excludes calculators, cash registers and typewriters with a small display screen.)

Regulation 2 – risk analysis

This requires that the employer carries out a workstation assessment. This assessment must be a suitable and sufficient analysis to assess the health and safety risks the users may be exposed to as a result of using the equipment. It must include all workstations used by employees regardless, of who actually provided them.

The assessment should identify the risks in the *work space*:

- Is the workstation designed and positioned so that the user is able to change position?
- Is the room lighting satisfactory and does it provide adequate contrast?
- Are there reflections and glare?
- What levels of noise are emitted by the equipment?
- What levels of heat are generated by the equipment?
- Are there more than negligible levels of radiation, other than those in the visible part of the electromagnetic spectrum?
- Are adequate humidity levels established and maintained?

It should also assess the *interfaces*:

- Is the software suitable for the task?
- Is the software easy to use and, where appropriate, can it be adapted to the level of knowledge or experience of the operator?
- Does the software provide feedback to the operator on performance of those systems?
- Does the software display information in a format and at a pace that can be adapted to meet the needs of the operator?

This assessment will often identify a number of areas for concern, and these will need further evaluation and corrective action to reduce the risks.

The codes of practice identify three general categories of risk to health:

Bad posture

- Most of these risks may be overcome by simple adjustments to ways of working.
- This will often highlight the need for training.

Damage to eyesight

- These risks may need only simple remedies such as repositioning of the equipment or the use of blinds.
- Glare and reflections can be prevented by co-ordinating workplace and workstation artificial light.

Fatigue and stress

- These risks may be reduced by considering the design of workstations.
- Remedies will often involve reviewing rest periods or the pace of work.

Regulation 3: new workstations

The employer must ensure that **all** workstations meet the requirements laid down in the schedules to the regulations.

Regulation 4: breaks

The employer is required to organise the activities of users so that their daily work using display screen equipment is regularly interrupted by breaks or changes of activity to reduce their continuous workload at that equipment.

The codes of practice recommend that:

* breaks should be taken *before* fatigue sets in and not to recuperate from it
* frequent short breaks are preferable, eg 5–10 minutes every hour
* breaks should be taken *away* from the display screen.

Jobs that involve a mixture of screen and non-screen work may well have sufficient breaks away from the screen to make scheduled breaks unnecessary.

Regulation 5: eyes and eyesight

If you are a regular, substantial user of display screen equipment or about to become one, you are entitled to ask for eye and eyesight tests. They must be carried out as soon as practicable by a competent person and usually before you become a user. Thereafter regular check-ups can be requested.

Where it is found that you need special corrective appliances (usually special spectacles) the cost of these has to be borne by the employer. It does not cover persons who need normal eyesight correction, but only where a special type is required to deal specifically with a problem in using VDUs.

Regulation 6: provision of training

Where an employee is a user or is about to become a user, the employer must ensure that:

* the employee is provided with adequate health and safety training in the use of any workstation upon which he or she may be required to work
* whenever there is any substantial modification to the workstation the user must be provided with adequate health and safety training.

Regulation 7: provision of information

The employer must ensure that:

* all users are provided with adequate information about all aspects of health and safety relating to their workstation
* users are informed of measures taken by the employer in compliance with duties under Regulation 2 (assessment) and Regulation 3 (workstations) as relate to them and their work.

Good practice when working with VDUs

There are many examples of good practice which can reduce risks to the health of VDU users. You will need to make sure that you adopt these safe working practices yourself and encourage and support those you are responsible for to do so as well.

Figure 7 shows correct posture when seated at a workstation and the positioning of the equipment in relation to the user.

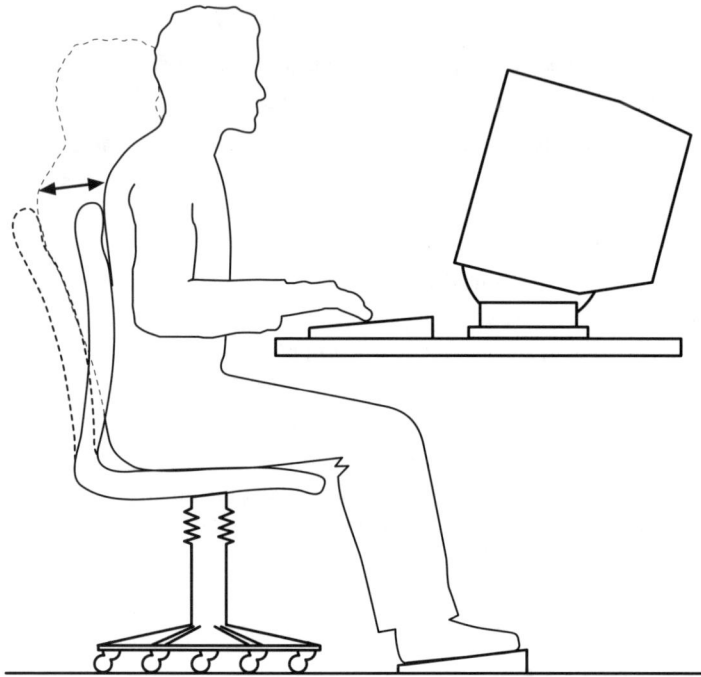

Figure 7   *Correct posture for sitting at a workstation*

One of the most important aspects of the computer workstation is that it should be adjustable to fit you or whoever is working there. When you get into the driving seat of a car you adjust the seating position for comfort and safe access to the controls. You, and your staff, should do the same when you sit down at your workstation.

Always check the following:

The height of the chair
* there should be sufficient space below the desk top to be able to move your legs freely

- a foot rest may be needed so that the back of the users' legs and knees do not have excess pressure on them
- arms should be horizontal and the users' eyes should be on a level with the top of the VDU.

The support provided by the chair
- support should be provided for the back, but without undue pressure.

Mobility of the sitting position
- sitting in the same position for too long should be avoided
- the user needs to be able to move the position of the chair with ease in relation to the workstation and the different tasks likely to be carried out.

The image on the screen
- the brightness and contrast should be adjusted so that they are comfortable for the user – the image should be sharply focused and easy to read
- the screen should be cleaned regularly, as dirt and finger marks distort the image
- appropriate colour schemes should be used wherever possible.

The layout of the workstation
- the keyboard, mouse mat, mouse and monitor should be moved to meet the work needs
- the installation of the mouse can be amended to accommodate left and right handedness
- the keyboard should be adjusted so that the user does not need to bend his or her hands up at the wrists
- there should be sufficient space for papers, disk boxes etc. If the user frequently works from paper documents a document holder may improve the comfort of the workstation. A cluttered workspace will make for reduced productivity as well as fatigue.

The lighting conditions in the room
- bright lights should not reflect on the screen – you may need blinds to reduce sunlight at certain times of the day
- the location of the workstation needs to take into account both natural and artificial lighting
- there should be sufficient light on the papers the user is working from.

RSI (repetitive strain injury)

This is a condition from which quite a number of people suffer. It is an extremely painful and sometimes quite debilitating injury. It is most likely to occur in people who are carrying out small, rapid, movements of the hands, fingers and wrists. It would appear to be something that can be brought about by incorrect posture at the keyboard or excessive use without rest. Typists on old typewriters were less likely to get it because the range of movement required to operate a manual keyboard was much greater. Using a mouse, particularly for long periods of time without a break, can also be a cause.

The best thing for you to do, particularly if you use a keyboard or mouse for long periods at a time, is to make sure that:

- you have set the keyboard so that it is most comfortable for you
- that you position your hands correctly over the keys
- that you take suitable breaks.

CHECK IT YOURSELF

A workstation risk assessment of the working environment should be carried out on a regular basis. Using the checklist on page 28, organise a full risk assessment of your working environment and of those you are responsible for. Carry out any changes that are within your own authority, and make recommendations for other deficiencies to an appropriate person. Make sure that all of these are documented and put a copy in your evidence folder as supplementary evidence.

Health and safety checklist 1

Section 1: accidents	
Is there a formal procedure for reporting accidents? If yes, place a copy in your evidence folder	Yes ☐ No ☐
What information is recorded in the accident record book?	details of the injured person ☐
	details of the injury ☐
	details of the accident
	date ☐
	time ☐
	place ☐
	what happened ☐
	treatment received ☐
	name of witness (if any) ☐
Details of responsible person	name:
	job title:
Section 2: first aid	
What is the name of your nearest first aider? How can you contact him or her?	
What is kept in your nearest first aid box?	individually wrapped sterile bandages ☐
	sterile eye pads ☐
	triangular bandages ☐
	safety pins ☐
	eye bath ☐
	sterile water for eye baths ☐
	sterile wound dressings in different sizes ☐
	other:
Section 3: evacuation	
Name of responsible person	
Date and time of last evacuation drill you took part in	

Health and safety checklist 2: workstation risk assessment

	Yes	No
Screen		
Is the screen large enough?		
Is the image stable and flicker-free?		
Can you adjust the image so that it is sharply focused?		
Can you adjust the colour scheme to suit your needs?		
Can you adjust the angle of the screen?		
Keyboard		
Is the keyboard of an appropriate size?		
Can you feel or hear the keys when pressed?		
Is there sufficient space to arrange it to suit your needs?		
Workstation		
Is your chair comfortable?		
Is the seat height and tilt adjustable?		
Is the height of the back-rest adjustable?		
Is the back-rest adjustable to fit your back?		
Does the chair swivel?		
Is the chair mobile?		
Have you been given information on adjusting your chair?		
Do you have sufficient leg room?		
Can you adjust the height of the desk top?		
Do you need a foot rest?		
Is a foot rest provided?		
Is a document holder available?		
Do you have sufficient work space?		
Working environment		
Is there excessive glare in the work area?		
Are there reflections on your screen from the window?		
Are blinds fitted in the room?		
Are the lights too bright?		
Do you need more directed lighting?		
Is the desk top too shiny?		

Information about the company Autoware has been included in the form of a case study on pp. 157–62. It describes the nature and structure of the organisation and will provide you with a context in which to carry out this task. It is therefore essential that you read this before you attempt this activity.

Autoware occupies offices on three floors of a 1960s-style office block. The company will be moving to a new, high-tech building in three months' time. It will be the sole occupant of the building which is organised on two floors only with lift access to the upper floor. All areas will be cabled for computer and Internet access.

1. There are many health and safety considerations of the work environment that affect the well-being of the staff. Autoware has requested an advisory report on these issues so that the company can ensure that it will be creating a pleasant and safe working environment for its employees. Produce this report, paying particular attention to the IT issues.

2. Health and safety in the working environment is only successfully implemented where the staff are fully trained. Design a one-hour training session for Autoware staff on 'Reducing Risks in the Workplace'. This should include a programme and a presentation to support the delivery of the session.

Unit 301 Select and Enable Information Technology for Use

This unit contains three elements:

301.1 Select and configure equipment for use
301.2 Use equipment and resources effectively
301.3 Control the conclusion of information technology use.

You need to demonstrate that you can select equipment and make any necessary connections and configurations. You will also need to demonstrate that as you work with the equipment you comply with regulations and avoid damage to the working environment. You will need to show that you monitor resources and equipment use, initiating corrective action to resolve any equipment problems. You must also demonstrate that you can manage the storage of both data files and consumables.

To meet the requirements of this unit you should have a good understanding of the factors influencing the selection of particular equipment to be used. You will need to understand the importance of the manufacturer's instructions, particularly with regard to connection and configuration of the equipment and have a good grasp of the technical detail associated with using the installed operating and application software. You will also need to know the relevant content of current legislation and organisational procedures for your working environment.

The computer system

A computer system consists of both the hardware (the physical devices) and the software (the programs that enable it to function). The description of all of these components is known as the *systems specification*. It is extremely important that you know the specification of the system that you are using and have a good understanding of each of the components and how they work together.

The hardware

The hardware will include equipment for data capture, data processing, data storage and data output. You need to know about the different types of devices available and how to connect them together to form the computer system.

Data capture (input) devices

The input device is used to enter data into a computer system so that the data can be processed, stored if appropriate, and the resulting information can be made available to the user as output.

The keyboard

The computer keyboard is still one of the main devices used to input data. The standard keyboard has keys arranged in the same format as a typewriter, known as a QWERTY keyboard. There are, however, a number of additional keys on a computer keyboard. There will be a Control key (CTRL) and an Alternate key (ALT), with usually two of each – one on each side of the keyboard. They are similar in use and concept to the shift key found on any typewriter keyboard, that is they are used in conjunction with another key to modify the meaning of the key. There will be a set of Function keys across the top of the keyboard, usually 12 of them numbered F1 to F12. They are used by the different software applications to carry out particular actions. There will be a number of navigation keys, usually to the right of the main keys. These keys enable you to move up, down, left and right, and will also include Home and End keys. To the right of these, there will frequently be an additional numeric keypad. This is in a format similar to a calculator and enables more rapid input of numerical data.

Over the years there have been a number of attempts to change the layout of the standard keyboard. The layout was designed for a typewriter rather than a computer and was intended for a much smaller group of specialist users. There are issues to do with health and safety, particularly regarding RSI (repetitive strain injury), associated with the layout of the keyboard. However, whilst companies like MicroSoft have designed a Natural keyboard, they are still not commonly in use.

For a number of specialist applications, the standard keyboard can be replaced with a concept keyboard. Where there are a limited number of possible input selections and they can all be anticipated, the concept keyboard can overcome both the need for keyboarding skills and minimise input error. In many restaurants and shops, there are keyboards with the images of the options available overlaying a touch-sensitive pad.

There are a number of factors to be considered when selecting a keyboard, e.g. whether a concept keyboard would be appropriate. It is also esssential to be aware of the needs of the users. The feel and responsiveness of a keyboard is very important. Most modern keyboards do not make any sound, and it can therefore be important for the system to be set up so that the computer makes the 'click' that indicates to the user that a key has been pressed.

Pointing devices

Most computer systems will also have some form of pointing device as a means of inputting data. This will usually be a mouse. A mouse is a hand-held device that the user moves across a flat surface, rolling a ball across censors to move a pointer on the screen. The mouse will usually have two, or sometimes three, buttons which are used to initiate actions based on the positioning of the pointer. These buttons may need to be held down as the mouse is dragged, single-clicked or double-clicked. A mouse is an essential device when working in an environment using a graphical user interface.

There are a number of variations to the mouse that have been developed. The tracker ball is like an upside-down mouse, with the ball on the top of the device and with buttons in much the same way. The user simply moves the ball with his or her fingers to position the pointer. As the mouse is an external device which needs to be added to the computer system, particularly on lap-top computers, a range of alternatives to the mouse have been developed. There may be a variation of the tracker ball, which is usually placed in the centre of the keyboard and more recently there has been the introduction of a small, touch-sensitive pad with buttons similar to a mouse.

There are a number of alternative pointing devices that can be used, usually for specific types of application or environment:

- Digitising tablet – this works by using a stylus that is drawn over the tablet. It is capable of far greater precision than a mouse and is therefore used in engineering and drawing environments.
- Light pen – this works by moving across the screen and uses a light-sensitive tip to track its movement. It can only be used with CRT (cathode ray tube) screens and cannot be used with lap-top computers.
- Touch screen – this works by the user touching different areas of the screen to indicate their selection. It is particularly appropriate in systems that are available to the general public where other input devices are not necessary, eg public information systems.

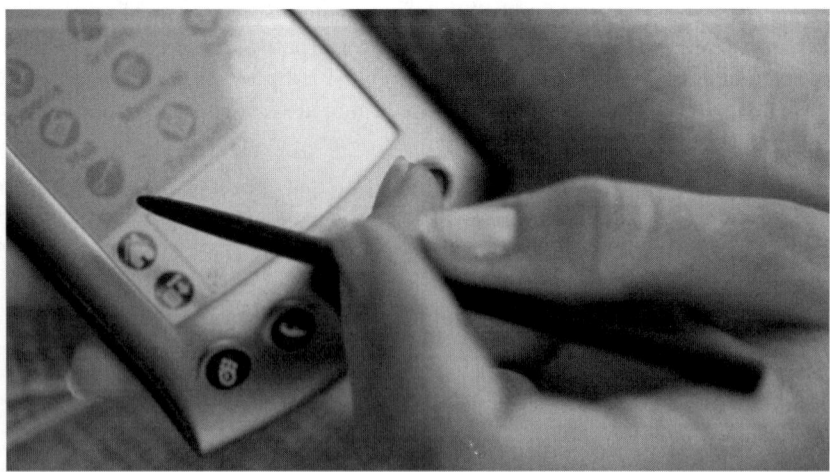

Figure 8   *A light pen*

Sensors

Some computer systems capture the data by detecting activity in the operational environment. This data takes the form of continuously varying values such as temperature, light, pressure, sound or humidity and will be analogue in form. This type of data cannot be used directly by most computer systems and will need to be converted into digital form using an ADC device. A microphone is an example of a sensor. The sound waves received by the microphone are converted to electrical voltages which are then sampled and stored as binary code by the sound card. In a computer-controlled greenhouse, a temperature sensor will be used to collect changes in temperature at pre-determined intervals; these take the form of an electrical signal. These are then converted, by an ADC, into discrete digital values that can be understood by the computer.

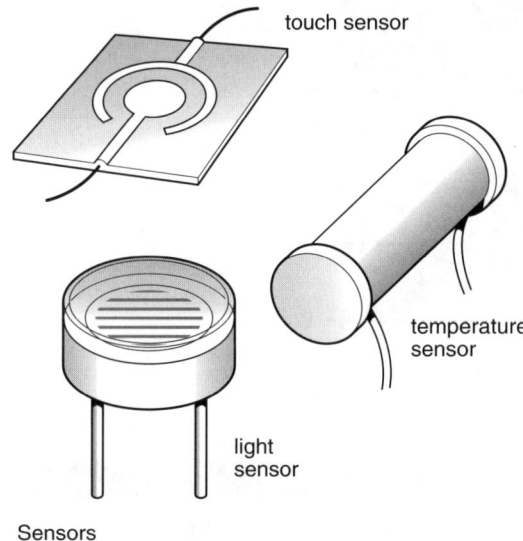

Sensors

Figure 9 *Types of sensors*

Scanners

Flat-bed scanner
A flat-bed scanner can be used to optically scan whole documents and convert the contents to a digital image. Text documents can be captured and converted into text format for use in a word processor by the use of optical character recognition (OCR) software.

Optical mark reader
An optical mark reader (OMR) reads pencil marks made in predefined positions on a piece of paper. These devices may be used to capture answers for multiple choice exam questions and in the selection of numbers for the national lottery.

Bar code reader

Bar codes are used to record data in a printed format that can also be read easily by a bar code reader, frequently a simple hand-held device. The bar code consists of variable width printed bars representing values and is particularly useful where the values are pre-set and should not be able to be altered. Many products purchased in a shop are labelled with a bar code which can be used to identify the product and therefore the price. This book has a bar code printed on the back cover to indicate the ISBN (the book's unique reference number).

Figure 10 *A bar code reader*

CHECK IT YOURSELF

Find out what input devices you have available on your system and any technical information. Record this in Section 1 of the systems specification checklist on p. 43 so that you can include this in your evidence folder as supplementary evidence.

Data processing equipment

Processor

This is the part of the computer that carries out all the instructions and is frequently identified in the model number of the computer; part of its description will include information about its speed. For example, you may be using a 486 66Mhz or perhaps a Pentium III 500MHz machine. As models and speeds of processors change so frequently, you need to find out what is considered to be the current 'entry level' model. Computer magazines are a good source of such information.

Memory

There are various parts of memory in a computer, each of which carries out a different function. The part that you, the user, needs to be most aware of is RAM (random access memory). This memory temporarily holds the programs and instructions you are using and the data that you input. This part of the computer's memory is usually 'volatile', that is, when you switch it off everything that has not been stored has gone.

CHECK IT YOURSELF

Find out the make, model, processor and speed of the computer you use most frequently. Record this in section 2 of the systems specification checklist on p. 43 so that you can include this in your evidence folder as supplementary evidence.

Data output devices

Visual display unit

One of the main output devices on a computer system is a video display unit, the VDU. It may also be referred to as the screen or monitor. It is used to communicate from the computer to the user; it will display information coming from the system but is also used to request data from the users, displaying the responses they make.

The technical specification of the VDU will include the size. This is a measurement, in inches, across the diagonal of the screen. Most personal computers will have a screen size of 14" or 15". However, particularly in a CAD or graphics environment, screen sizes of 17", 19" and 21" are more common as the level of detail is insufficient on the smaller screens.

The image on a screen is formed with pixels (picture elements) with each pixel forming one dot in an image. The display screen is organised as rows and columns of dots. The closer packed the pixels are, the sharper the quality of the image. The resolution of the screen indicates the number of pixels in each row and column, the greater the number of pixels, the higher the resolution. Any given monitor will have a maximum possible resolution, this maximum may also be reduced depending upon the number of colours to be used and the amount of memory on the graphics card. A resolution greater than 1024×768 on a screen smaller than 17" is not practical as the resulting image is too small.

The refresh rate of the screen determines how frequently the image is re-displayed. The more frequent the refresh, the less likely the user will detect any flicker. The rate of refresh is expressed as the number of times per second, a standard rate being 75 times every second, ie 75 Hz. When the screen is refreshed, the image is built up line by line. A non-interlaced monitor, which is the standard type, carries out this process as one scan, whereas with an interlaced monitor, the refresh takes place in two separate passes. Although the refresh takes longer with an interlaced monitor, it is rarely perceptible to the user in many applications but with complex graphics, animation and video it is likely to produce some flicker.

The majority of monitors have colour display, although monochrome monitors with one colour for background, usually black, and white, amber or green foreground are perfectly adequate for many situations. Colour is achieved through mixing red, green and blue in varying quantities. The more colours a screen can display, the more memory is required on the graphics card.

LCD (liquid crystal display) monitors are based on TFT (thin film transistor) technology resulting in flicker-free viewing. They are very much thinner than CRT (cathode ray tube) monitors, give off about a third as much heat and produce virtually no electromagnetic emissions. They are capable of high resolutions and can display many millions of colours. They are extremely compact and energy-efficient but currently are considerably more expensive than conventional CRT monitors.

Printers

The other main means of output is still on to paper. Although there has been much talk of the paperless office, we are still a long way from this. There are three main factors that need to be taken into account with printing requirements: quality, including colour; speed; and costs, both purchase and running costs.

The speed at which a printer works is usually expressed in ppm (pages per minute). This figure will not reflect the speed that any page is printed at, but will represent the number of average pages; a page with a considerable amount of graphics will take a lot longer. The quality of the print is described in dpi (dots per inch). The more dots, the higher the quality produced.

Laser printer

In the office environment, the laser printer is now probably the most common type of printer. The quality of output produced is very high and the costs are relatively low. A standard monochrome laser printer attached to a PC would probably operate at between 12 and 18 ppm with a resolution of 600dpi, although sometimes this may be as high 1200dpi. In a network environment, larger, faster laser printers may be used, with print speeds of up to 32 ppm at 600 dpi or even 50 ppm at 300dpi. Colour laser printers are capable of speeds between 2 and 5ppm at similar resolutions. These printers are still relatively expensive, but definitely the best colour printing solution if quality and speed are required, particularly without the need to use special paper.

Many laser printers are now capable of a range of finishing facilities more frequently associated with a photocopier. The more sophisticated printers can do double-sided printing, collating the document as required and stapling the finished product ready for distribution.

Ink jet printer

Ink jet printers are more commonly used for monochrome (and colour) printing on personal computers. However, for many organisations, where colour printing is not a regular requirement, this type of printer may be used for colour output. The speed of an ink jet printer is much less than a laser printer, typically printing at only 2 or 3 ppm. The resolution will usually be between 300 dpi and 700 dpi, but the best results are only achieved when this is combined with special quality paper.

Impact printer

This refers to all printers that produce the image on the page by striking the page through some sort of ink dispersing process, eg a ribbon. Examples of this type of printer include dot matrix printers, which use a matrix of pins to produce the printed information, and line printers which have a complete drum of available characters and print a whole line at a time. Whilst these printers are not suitable for high quality printing, and have limitations on what they can print, they are the only form of printing available where you need to use multi-part stationery. Some line printers work at speeds of up to 1500 lines per minute (lpm).

Plotter

Plotters are used to produce high quality output in a graphics environment, particularly for CAD applications. The image is created using a number of different coloured pens which are picked up and put down by an 'arm' which moves across the paper.

Sound card

This is an expansion board that enables the computer to capture and play high quality sound. It will include sockets for speakers to output the sound files and one for a microphone for input.

CHECK IT YOURSELF

Find out what output devices you have available on your system and any technical information. Record this in section 3 of the systems specification checklist on p. 43 so that you can include this in your evidence folder as supplementary evidence.

Data storage

Magnetic disk

The main storage medium in computer systems is the hard disk. This is a high-capacity storage device, storing many gigabytes of data. In a network environment there may be several file servers attached to provide the shared storage for all the users.

The floppy disk is still the main removable storage medium for most PC users. The standard floppy disk has a capacity of only 1.4Mbytes and, although still extremely useful for offline storage of some files, has ceased to be the main medium for distribution of software due to the limited capacity. There are a number of proprietary software tools available to compress data so that typically up to 15 or 20Mbytes of data can be stored on one 1.4Mb disk.

A number of other higher capacity magnetic disk drives have been introduced during the last ten years, although none has become an industry standard as the 3.5 floppy drive did. Examples of these are the Zip drive and the Jaz drive.

Magnetic tape

Magnetic tape is used exclusively as a backing storage system, usually in larger environments and for systems backups. Even the smallest QIC (quarter inch cartridges) have capacities of several gigabytes and can therefore often contain a full backup of a PC's hard drive.

Optical media

CDs have become the standard medium for storage of electronic material for distribution. The disks are far more robust than the floppy disk and have much greater capacity, with typical storage capacities of 650Mbytes. The CD is, however, a permanent storage medium which can be written to once only. The computers that you work with will typically have a CD drive which is only capable of reading data from a CD. However, CD-R (compact disk – recorder) is now become more freely available, providing the capability of writing to the CD.

More recently the DVD (digital video disk) has become available. Originally developed for recording video data, but with the ability to read CDs, DVDs with CD-R capability are frequently a standard feature of many PCs.

CHECK IT YOURSELF

What is the size of the hard disk in your computer? Do you have any other types of data storage media available to you? Record this in section 4 of the systems specification checklist on p. 43 so that you can include this in your evidence folder as supplementary evidence.

Connecting the hardware

Connecting up a personal computer is a relatively straightforward process. The workstation you and your colleagues use will probably be a PC which will then be connected to the network.

The main computer box, the system unit, is what the other devices are connected to. You will find most of the connectors at the back of the system unit and they will be labelled, either with words or images, to assist you in the process. If you have not connected up a system before, it is a good idea to do it the first time with an expert available to observe, advise and encourage.

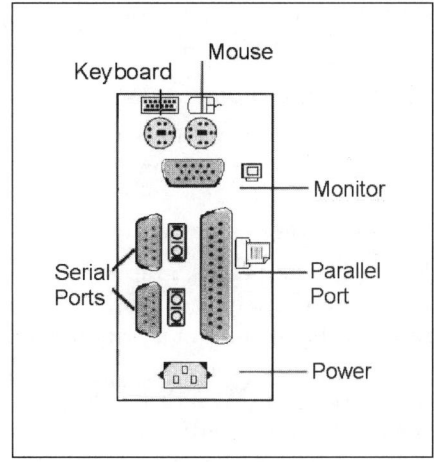

Figure 11 *Types of connectors*

Monitor connection

The monitor is connected to the system unit using a data cable; this cable will be permanently attached to the monitor and will have a 'D' connector at the end. This cable is plugged into the matching 'D' connector which will be labelled with 'Monitor' or something similar. The shape of the connector ensures that it is only possible to plug it in the right way round.

Keyboard connection

The keyboard is connected to the system unit using a permanently connected cable which ends in a round 6-pin connector. This is connected to the round female connector in the system unit. The connector has a tag which means it can only go in one way.

Mouse connection

A serial mouse is either connected either to the COM1 serial port at the back of the system unit using a 9-pin 'D' connector or to a round 6-pin connector similar to the keyboard. Sometimes you will connect to the second serial port, but this may require an adapter. The cable will be permanently fixed to the mouse.

Parallel printer connection

Most printers are connected to the systems unit using the parallel printer port, although some printers may use a serial connection. The printer cable will not be permanently connected to the printer. The connector on the cable to be plugged into the printer will be a 25-way **male** connector which connects to a 25-way **female** socket on the printer, the other end of the cable will have a 25-pin connector which connects to a 25-pin **female** socket on the systems unit.

Power connections

The system unit, printer and monitor will each have a separate power cable and these should be the last connections that you make. Each plug should be connected to a separate power socket; you should not use multi-way adapters.

Power-up/down procedures

You should check to make sure that all the connections have been correctly made before switching on the power.

Installing device drivers

Printers, sound cards, graphics cards, etc., need programs, known as drivers, to control the way they work. For example, an incorrect driver may result in some of the features of a printer not being available, or even worse the output could be complete rubbish. A new printer will be supplied with the necessary software on disk. This will come with instructions of how to run the program, but will often require you to run a setup.exe program. This will prompt you for any necessary information and then carry out the installation. You will usually need to restart the computer after the installation as it will have made changes to the configuration files.

Installing software

Software is usually supplied on CD with a set of instructions. Most installations are quite straightforward, with you following prompts for information such as the location of the programs and details of your licences. You will usually be required to supply company details for technical support from the supplier.

You will often be given a choice of type of installation, usually one option will be for a typical or standard installation which is the one recommended for all but the most experienced of users. If you choose to carry out a custom installation you will be able to ensure that all facilities that you require are installed and also to not install those that are not needed. It will be possible to update this installation at a later point, adding or removing a facility that was not originally installed.

On completion of the installation, you will usually need to restart the system. This is because the installation process has made modifications to the configuration files, identifying for the operating system that the program is installed and where the files are located.

It is absolutely essential that, when the installation is complete, you fully test the software to make sure that it operates correctly. You will need to be aware of the users' requirements and how the software integrates with the rest of the systems.

The software

Software is the word used to describe all computer programs. Systems software is used to enable the hardware to operate and applications software enables the computer to be used for a specific purpose, eg payroll, word processing or to play a game.

Systems software

The function of the operating system is to manage and communicate with the resources of the computer system. A simple operating system like MS-DOS is designed to run one program at a time for a single user. A multi-tasking system such as Windows 98 allows a user to have several programs loaded at one time, switching between them as needed. Networks are managed by a network operating system which controls the users' access to shared resources and manages the access rights of the users.

Utilities are programs, usually included with the operating system, which carry out routine maintenance tasks such as file management, disk management and disk repair on the computer system.

The BIOS (basic input/output system) holds the details of the hardware installed and the settings for each of the individual components. It is held in the CMOS RAM which only requires a very small amount of battery power to retain the information. The BIOS settings are used to control the system start-up when the computer is switched on and to carry out diagnostic tests on the hardware.

Programming languages such as Visual Basic, C++, Pascal, Java and Delphi are development tools. These are used to create software application solutions.

CHECK IT YOURSELF

What operating system do you have on your computer? What version number are you using? Is your computer connected to a network? If so, what is the network operating software? Record this in section 5 of the systems specification checklist on p. 44 so that you can include this in your evidence folder as supplementary evidence.

Applications software

Special purpose applications software is software that can only be used for the specific purpose for which it has been written, for example a payroll package can only be used for working out the pay of staff, it cannot be used for anything else. In some instances this type of software is available 'off-the-shelf' but may not always meet the precise needs of the user. Alternatively software will be created using development tools to provide a bespoke solution.

Generic – general purpose – software is software that can be used for a number of purposes. A spreadsheet package can be used for a wide variety of applications, particularly where manipulation of numbers is involved.

You will look in detail at a number of generic software packages for the optional units of the qualification.

CHECK IT YOURSELF

What applications software do you have access to? What version number are you using? Record this in section 5 of the systems specification checklist on p. 44 so that you can include this in your evidence folder as supplementary evidence.

Systems specification checklist

Section 1: input devices	
keyboard	
pointing devices	
sensors	
scanners	
other	
Section 2: processor	
make	
model	
processor	
processor speed	
RAM	
Section 3: output devices	
VDU	
printer:	
type	
make	
model	
speed	
quality	
sound card	
plotter	
other	
Section 4: storage devices	
hard disk	
floppy disk	
CD	
other	

Systems specification checklist (continued)

Section 5: software	
operating system:	
name	
version	
network software	
name	
version	
applications software	
type of application	
name	
version	
type of application	
name	
version	
type of application	
name	
version	
type of application	
name	
version	
type of application	
name	
version	

Case Study Activity

Information about the company Autoware has been included in the form of a case study on pp. 157–62. It describes the nature and structure of the organisation and will provide you with a context in which to carry out this task. It is therefore essential that you read this before you attempt this activity.

Autoware has a wide range of hardware and software to support the development and technical staff. There is also a significant network of computers that is used for the day-to-day running of the business, administration, finance, etc. There are a number of different types and models of printers being used throughout the organisation and this results in maintenance problems.

1. Carry out an investigation into the different printer options available and the relative quality and cost issues that each one presents. Produce a report for Gillian Bates, the Chief Executive, so that rationalisation can take place.

2. As the development staff frequently need to test software on different hardware configurations, they regularly require systems to be disconnected and re-connected. Due to very high workloads, this task is often carried out by non-technical staff and it would therefore be very useful if these staff had a simple set of instructions on the procedure. Write a procedure that will take them through the basic process, using your IT skills to ensure a well-presented and 'user friendly' document.

Unit 302 Maintain the Software Environment

This unit contains three elements:

302.1 Specify and maintain file structures
302.2 Update installed software
302.3 Establish and control media and documentation storage.

You need to demonstrate that you can set up and manage appropriate file organisation structures for yourself and your colleagues, to include security backup procedures and records. You will also need to demonstrate that you can make modifications to the installed software, installing updates whilst ensuring the effective performance of the system for both yourself and your colleagues.

To meet the requirements of this unit you will need to have a wide appreciation of the file storage requirements of the organisation to enable you to specify, design and document the structures to be used. You should have a good understanding of the factors that affect data security requirements and the importance of accurate backup records. You will need to understand the factors affecting the storage of data media and associated documentation. You will also need to know how to carry out installation updates in line with manufacturer's guidelines and understand the impact such updates may have on others and the performance of the systems.

File structures

Almost everything that is created using a computer that needs to be kept is stored in a file – the software you buy, the data you input, the letters and memos you type, and even most of the operating systems that you use to make the computer work. These files are stored in folders or directories on a storage device.

Whatever computer system you are using, there will be a set of rules, controlled by the operating system, about the names you give to files and how you organise the storage.

If you are using an industry-standard PC, you will probably be using a version of Microsoft Windows or NT. If you are using a different operating system you will need to find out the rules that apply to your computer.

Filenames

Every file has to have a name. This name must be unique to the storage area, folder or directory. The name must usually consist of only letters and numbers – many of the other characters on a keyboard have a special meaning in a filename. Files created in a Windows 95, or later, environment have two parts. The first part is given by the user, can also include spaces and can have up to 255 characters. The end of the first part of the name is indicated by the use of the full stop (.). This can then be followed by a second part, sometimes called the extension or suffix. This consists of up to 3 characters and will often be given automatically to the file by the specific application software, eg word processing documents often have a suffix of **doc**. The complete filename is recorded in a folder, or directory, and is used to access the file. The directory contains details about the file, usually the date and time it was created or last updated, where it is located on the disk and what size (in bytes) it is.

Folders (directories) and sub-folders

When a disk is first used in a computer it has to be set up; this is known as formatting. Part of the disk is set aside to hold the directory information necessary to locate the files on the disk. This is known as the root folder/directory and is referenced by the drive letter; a colon (:) and the back slash (\). For example the root directory of the first floppy disk drive is referenced by A:\ . As it is possible to have a large number of files on any one disk, it is extremely important to organise them into sub-folders so that you can find them easily.

The system of subdirectories is hierarchical and is best understood through the diagram given in Figure 12. The paths in Figure 12 are written as (i) A:\aa, (ii) A:\bb, (iii) A:\cc, (iv) A:\dd, (v) A:\bb\ee and (vi) A:\bb\ff. Thus if all your documents relating to a sports and social club are stored on a floppy disk in subdirectory cc, you would find the minutes of the last committee meeting at A:\cc\mins200.

Data storage standards

The files that are created and stored whilst at work belong to the organisation. This means that they need to be accessible to authorised people within the organisation. Would you be able to find a document created by the staff you are responsible for so that you could print a copy or make some amendments when they are on holiday or off sick or if they leave the organisation?

Data storage standards need to include the following:

- file naming conventions
- filing systems
- recording systems.

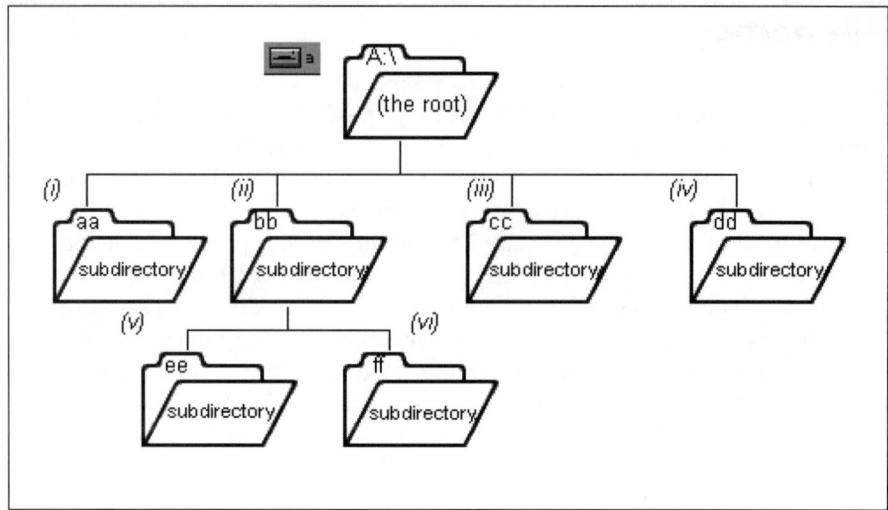

Figure 12 *Disk structure*

File naming conventions

There need to be guidelines or rules as to what names are given to files. When working with most operating systems this can be quite difficult. As you should have found out, there are many rules and limitations about what names you can give to your files. You may also have found out how difficult it can be to find the file you want several weeks or months after you have created it. Many organisations will have their own set of rules about naming of files. This is particularly important for the files that are stored for access by a number of users, but there will frequently also be a set of conventions, which may be informally agreed, that are followed within an office or team.

The file name will need to include information about content, author, operator and version. The date is not necessary as this is held within the directory.

Filing systems

There needs to be guidelines or rules about where the files are stored. It may be almost impossible to find your files unless they are organised into subdirectories or folders but, like any filing system, it is important that others can find their way round as well as you. Again, it is particularly important where files need to be available to more than one user.

You have been given responsibility for reviewing and revising the file storage structure within your organisation.

Design an appropriate set of rules for filenames, directory names and directory structures. You will need to produce a document to explain this information to your staff and colleagues.

Recording systems

Not only must these first two rules be adhered to but also the details of the files and the structure of your filing system need to be recorded. All systems require some sort of documentation. Just because data is held and organised on a computer does not mean that documentation is no longer necessary – in fact, in many respects it becomes more critical as most of your main filing system and data are electronically stored. It is often not as easy to scan quickly through a computer system to find the file you need as with one on paper.

Let us say that your team creates, on average, between 100 and 150 new files a day. After working for a period of six months the team could have created over 5000 files! If you, or anyone else, wanted to find a document created five months ago, where would you start?

Many of these documents may have been amended or updated and sometimes you could have kept different versions for reference purposes. How will you know which version to use? To avoid wasting a considerable amount of time searching through your filing system it is important to maintain an easy-to-use recording system.

Large volumes of data and a considerable number of different files can be contained both online (stored on disks that are permanently connected to the computer) and offline (stored on disks that need to be loaded). There need to be records so that they can be easily located. What if the owner is not in the office? What happens when someone leaves the organisation? External bodies such as auditors also need to be able to find them, and so on.

For some of these records you can use the computer to produce the information. Printouts can give folder details for all disks (Figure 13). A procedure is needed to specify how often these records are updated and where they are stored.

Name	Size	Type	Modified
206.doc	86KB	Micro...	03/12/01 00:5
301.doc	73KB	Micro...	03/12/01 00:4
303.doc	41KB	Micro...	03/12/01 01:0
311.doc	336KB	Micro...	02/12/01 20:4
312.doc	53KB	Micro...	03/12/01 00:2
326.doc	102KB	Micro...	02/12/01 12:0
327.doc	113KB	Micro...	02/12/01 18:1
Jobs.doc	110KB	Micro...	02/12/01 23:5
letterpen.doc	20KB	Micro...	26/07/01 10:4
Rachel.doc	20KB	Micro...	11/12/01 07:1

Figure 13 *Folder details*

CHECK IT YOURSELF

Based on the newly specified file storage structure, you now need to produce a set of rules specifying the documentation required to support this system. This will need to include the methods used, how and where stored and the frequency required.

Storage of data media

The off-line data storage media such as floppy disks, CDs, tapes, etc., need to be stored in an appropriate environment. Data media, whether floppy disks, DVDs, CDs, etc. contain valuable data and need to be stored correctly. All media storage should avoid:

- excessive heat
- excessive light
- magnetic fields
- dust
- bending and crushing
- damp
- flooding or spillage.

The organisation of this storage is extremely important. Disks, and their boxes, sleeves, etc. need to be clearly and accurately labelled. This needs to indicate the content, the owner and the date. Paper records will also need to be kept where there are high volumes, so that they can be more easily located.

The physical organisation of the media is important. How many desks in your work area have floppy disks or CDs on them? Appropriate storage boxes need to be used, and clearly labelled.

Security

The more an organisation is dependent upon a computer system, the more vulnerable it is should the system fail. The organisation will need to consider disaster recovery management and identify potential problem areas, including:

- physical security – the environment where processing activities are carried out must be secure
- personnel security – staff could reveal passwords, take advantage of access or be subject to personal threats
- hardware security – equipment could be stolen, power failure could occur, computers could be damaged by viruses
- communications security – data could be intercepted during transmission between sites or across the Internet
- software security – software needs to be robust (ie cannot be copied).

Each of these problem areas can be overcome by some form of backup or protection. However, each extra step taken to secure the system will add to the cost of the system.

To assess the extent of the vulnerability and be able to decide what level of protection is required, the organisation needs to carry out a risk analysis.

The risk analysis would need to consider the following points:

- What is the likelihood of the disaster?
- How long might the disaster be in effect?
- What would happen to the data in the event of this disaster?
- How quickly could the system recover when the disaster is over?
- What are the costs to the organisation in terms of data recovery?
- What are the costs to the organisation in terms of lost business?
- What are the costs to the organisation in terms of staff morale?
- What are the costs of installing the backup and/or protection system?
- Do the financial losses outweigh the costs of the solution?

Data backup and recovery procedures

A backup is a secure copy of your data files. If your original files are damaged or lost, you can recover the files from the backup copy.

In many operating systems, as well as being able to make copies of a file, there will be a backup command or function. You can back up the files on your system on to floppy disks, a tape drive, or another computer on your network. The resulting back-up file may be placed on more than one disk or tape, depending upon its size. It will also contain a backup control file that identifies the date and time and, where it is on more than one disk and the sequence of the disks.

The restore command is the other half of the procedure. This command enables you to restore some or all of the data from these disks. It uses the information in the control file to find the data and to prompt the operator through the process.

These commands will usually allow you to carry out the backup procedure in a number of different ways. You can back up or restore:

- all the files in a directory/folder
- all the files in a directory/folder and any subdirectories/folders of that directory
- only those files that have been updated or created on or after a specified date/time
- only those files updated or created since the last backup.

During the process you can:

- overwrite all previous files or
- add files to those already on a backup file.

Documentation

Backup and archiving procedures must have permanent records to enable them to function correctly. Backup details need to be logged and tapes or disks need to be labelled appropriately. You need to know when the latest backup was taken and what updates have taken place if you are going to be able to restore your records in the event of some form of disaster.

A backup strategy needs to be designed to cope with potential data loss. It is absolutely essential to ensure that adequate backups are taken at critical intervals and that they are stored securely, preferably in different locations.

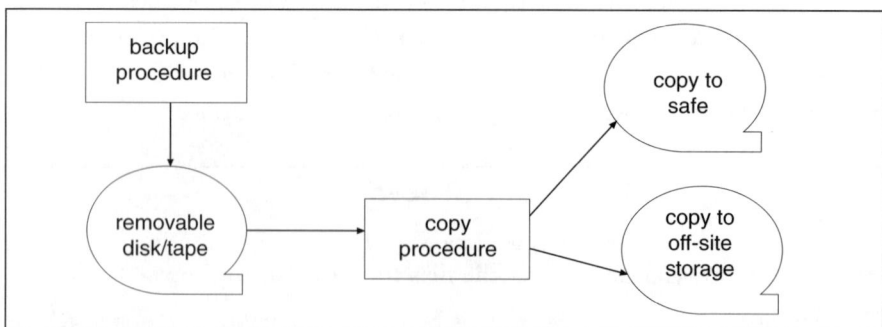

Figure 14 *Backup procedure*

Protection of data

The systems and the data need protection to ensure their security. There will need to be protection against the following:

1) The physical loss or damage to equipment and data
   a) This could arise through natural disaster (flooding, fire, etc.), through equipment failure or through malicious and deliberate action to steal or damage the machines.
   b) Protection against natural disasters is quite difficult. You can make sure that, wherever possible, the equipment is kept in less vulnerable locations. Appropriate fire warning systems will need to exist together with fire-fighting precautions in line with manufacturer's recommendations.
   c) Protection against equipment failure can be met, to some extent, through adequate maintenance cover.
   d) The portability of so much equipment increases the chances of theft. Physical security can be provided by methods as simple as fixing down the equipment, so that it cannot be moved. You should, wherever possible, locate equipment in a secure and protected environment.

2) Unauthorised access to the system resulting in copying or viewing of data or software
   a) This could arise through hacking or unauthorised disclosure.
   b) Physical protection can be provided through limited access to the location. This could be by the use of security personnel or locked rooms.
   c) Logical protection can be provided through password protected access to the systems.

3) Unauthorised access to the system resulting in corruption of the data or software
   a) This could arise through malicious or accidental action. Inadequately trained staff or poorly designed systems could result in errors being made. This could also arise through intentional action, either for personal gain, theft, or wilful destruction of data or software as a form of industrial espionage.

b) Physical protection can be provided through limited access to the location. This could be by the use of security personnel or locked rooms.

c) Logical protection can be provided through password protected access to the systems.

Many organisations are reluctant to report or publicise the extent to which some of these activities take place because of the damage it could do to their credibility. Most organisations will have some level of security for access to the buildings and the staff work areas (particularly if it is a place that is open to the general public) and the computer systems will be made secure mainly through passwords and location of equipment.

However, much of the unauthorised access is brought about through failure to follow procedures. How easy is it to 'talk your way in' to the building where you work or study, or walk in unchallenged? How secure are your passwords?

CHECK IT YOURSELF

Investigate the security systems in your organisation and produce a report describing the procedures. Review the operation of these procedures within your area of work and produce a second report on their effectiveness, identifying areas of improvement. Place copies of these reports in your folder as supplementary evidence.

Update of software

Software, particularly proprietary packages, are updated on a regular basis. At some point it may be necessary for your organisation to upgrade to the latest version. This may arise because the additional facilities of the latest version will improve or extend the use of the system, or because the earlier version is no longer supported, or because other systems changes mean that the latest version is required.

The procedures for an update of the software will often be similar to those of a full installation, but will usually be almost entirely automated through an *install* program. You will need to have details of the previous installation, possibly including licence details and information about where, which drive and folder, the programs are currently stored.

You will need to carry out a full set of tests after the installation is complete to make sure that full functionality is available and that nothing has been lost to the users. The last thing you want is for the users to be able to do less with the upgrade than they could before! You will need to draw up a test plan to ensure that nothing is omitted. This will need to test all the functions that are currently used. For example, with a new version of the word processing software you might request examples of all the different types of documents produced. You could then re-produce each of these, checking the results against the originals.

Any decision to update software will need to be made taking into account the impact this may have on the existing systems. Will you need greater storage capacity, will the other applications be able to link correctly with this new version, will you need to update other applications to ensure compatibility?

You will also need to consider the impact it will have on other users. A new version of a piece of software, whilst still having the same capability, may have a very different look and feel to it. To the inexperienced user this can be very upsetting. It is essential that any upgrade takes place with the full knowledge of all users, is planned around other users' work patterns and appropriate training is included.

Case Study Activity

Information about the company Autoware has been included in the form of a case study on pp. 157–62. It describes the nature and structure of the organisation and will provide you with a context in which to carry out this task. It is therefore essential that you read this before you attempt this activity.

The latest version of the e-mail software used in the organisation is going to be installed. This will obviously affect all users, as it is the primary means of communication within the organisation.

Draw up a training programme to be delivered at departmental level during the week before changeover to the new system.

Data file recovery strategy checklist

Systems backup	
person responsible	
written procedure?	
frequency of backup	
backup medium	
backup storage – on site	
backup storage – off site	
backup records	
Systems file recovery	
person responsible	
written procedure	
estimated time	
alternative system available?	
Local backup	
person responsible	
written procedure?	
frequency of backup	
backup medium	
backup storage	
backup records	
training provided?	
Local recovery	
written procedure?	
person responsible	
estimated time	
training provided?	

Case Study Activity

Information about the company Autoware has been included in the form of a case study on pp. 157–62. It describes the nature and structure of the organisation and will provide you with a context in which to carry out this task. It is therefore essential that you read this before you attempt this activity.

The administrative support staff within the development department work for a considerable number of people. In addition to the managers in the department, there are five members of the development team.

1. They will create letters, memos, reports, technical specifications and user manuals, all of which need to be stored on the network in the appropriate folders. You need to devise a file storage system that will accommodate all these requirements. Produce a structure diagram to show this.

2. Autoware does not have a written backup and recovery procedure. It takes nightly backups of all its network files and a copy is stored in the safe. A second copy is deposited in the bank safe. However, many staff also store data on the local hard drive and there are no guidelines as to backups for these.

    *   Produce a written backup strategy for the network system.
    *   Produce a set of guidelines for all staff regarding backup and storage for local hard drives.

Unit 303 Develop and Maintain the Effectiveness of the Information Technology Working Environment

This unit contains four elements:

303.1 Plan and organise the effective use of information technology

303.2 Provide informal information technology support to colleagues

303.3 Make recommendations for improvements

303.4 Implement improvements to the information technology working environment.

You need to demonstrate that you can plan and organise the availability and suitability of information technology resources, using appropriate planning aids, to meet the organisation's objectives, informing relevant people of any unresolved issues and their effects on the progress of the work. You will need to show that you can provide information and assistance to resolve problems for colleagues within the limits of your job responsibility. You will need to demonstrate that you regularly review the use of resources and the working environment, making recommendations for areas for improvement taking into account developments in the technology. You will also need to demonstrate that you have implemented improvements to the information technology environment.

To meet the requirements of this unit you should have a good understanding of the importance of prioritising work, monitoring and maintaining the equipment and keeping the relevant people informed. You will need to appreciate the scope and the limits of your IT capabilities, knowing when to refer requests for support to a relevant person. You will also understand the importance of keeping up to date with information relating to both the current installed hardware and software and other developments. You will need to know the relevant content of current legislation and manufacturer's instructions for your working environment and you will need to understand the importance of the potential effects of changes on others and the need to keep colleagues informed.

Planning and organising tools

In most current operating environments, there will usually be a number of planning and personal organising tools available. These are provided to assist you in the organisation of your work and the management of your use of the technology.

Calendar

There will be a diary, or calendar, system. This will enable you, and others, to record events and activities that need to take place. You can use it to schedule your workload and to organise meetings, etc., with others. It can also be set up to support your daily routine. For example, first thing in the morning, when you start up your computer, it will go to your diary and show you all the e-mails and faxes that you have received, possibly linking to your voicemail system, and listing all the tasks and activities scheduled for the day.

The diary system, in a fully networked environment can be a very powerful tool. How many hours have you spent trying to find a mutually convenient time to have a meeting with four or five other people in the organisation? Even using an e-mail system, with the possibility of fairly rapid response from all concerned, it can still be a slow and tedious process. With a diary system, it can be possible to immediately identify all the possible time-slots and then to agree the preferences of the other attendees.

Address book

There will also be an electronic address book system available. This will usually be a lot more than just a store of contacts' names and addresses. It will enable you to keep all the relevant contact details, including e-mail address, telephone number, and other key information about them. It can be used directly to make contact with them, by e-mail or through mailing labels, and will link into the calendar system.

Task manager

Task management software can be used to assist you with the various activities that you have to carry out. A task is a personal or work-related activity that you want to track through to completion. A task can occur once or repeatedly (a recurring task). A recurring task can repeat at regular intervals or to be repeated, based on the date you last completed the task. For example, you might want to send a status report to your manager on the last Friday of every month, and send out a marketing e-mail one month after the last one was sent.

Project management

Project management software goes a step further. This type of software is there to let you plan, in detail, a task or set of tasks. You can plan a project against time, resources and finances using such software. Most activities in an information technology environment are projects, that is, they are finite. It is therefore possible to identify start and end dates, and to break down the task into sub-tasks.

As each part of the project is completed, this can be recorded so that you can monitor and report on the progress to date. The software will assist you by producing a critical path analysis, identifying where delays in the completion of a sub-task could adversely affect the completion date of the project.

User support

There are a number of sources of support for computer users. Most generic software, and many of the custom-built applications, have some form of on-line help system.

User manuals vary considerably in their quality and usefulness. These manuals are now often provided as a text file that can be viewed and printed if necessary, or are available on the supplier's website ready to download when, and if, required. However, many users find it extremely useful to have their own set of guidelines or instructions that relate specifically to the parts of the system that they use and the way in which they use them.

You may find that one of the ways that you will need to support other users is by providing them with this sort of user guide.

What makes a good user guide?

User friendly

A user guide must be written to meet the specific needs of the user. It needs to describe the system and how to use it, from the *user's* perspective.

The language needs to be simple, clear, accurate and unambiguous; it should not be open to misinterpretation. The terminology should be familiar to the user.

The guide needs to be structured, it will rarely be used from start to finish because users will usually need to refer to it for those tasks they are not sure of, rather than all of it. This is best achieved by organising it into sections that are clearly separated so users can find the part they need quickly.

Most of the time users will want to use the guide as they work with the system. This means that step-by-step instructions are most useful. It is also helpful to provide 'screen-shots' so they can see on paper what they see on the screen.

The sequence needs to be the most likely order of use, although each section must be able to be used on its own.

Well presented

All the style factors that relate to any document apply to your guides. You need to ensure consistency of style and presentation.

It can be helpful to adopt a set of presentation rules such as, 'All instructions will appear in bold. All options will appear in italics.' This can help to remove ambiguity about what needs to be input and what needs to be responded to.

Do not put too much on a page; white space is an important design factor when creating this type of document.

Your guide will need a contents page and an index to make it easy to find a specific piece of information.

Other support

The other main support that you are most likely to provide will be on an ad-hoc basis. A colleague will need to carry out a task using a software feature he or she has not used before, someone carries out an activity only rarely and cannot remember what to do, or a fault has arisen and, before calling user support, has asked you to assist. It is important that you provide support only in those areas that you are competent; do not be afraid to pass on to someone better qualified.

Always keep a record of the level and type of support provided. This can be extremely useful; it is information that can be used to inform a planned staff training programme.

CHECK IT YOURSELF

What levels of user support are you responsible for? How many staff do you regularly support? Do you support the hardware, software, and other resources? The user support checklist on p. 64 includes all the main issues for user support. As you progress through the qualification, complete the checklist so that you can include this in your evidence folder as supplementary evidence.

Areas for improvement

Maintenance

An effective information technology environment is dependent upon appropriate and timely maintenance. Various aspects of the environment will work more efficiently with **planned** maintenance taking place, for example floppy disk drives need to be cleaned regularly to ensure effective operation – do not wait until they are not reading disks to clean them.

There will be occasions when **corrective** maintenance needs to take place. This is where a problem has occurred, for example the word processing software is no longer available through an icon on the desktop. This could easily arise where the user has accidentally erased the shortcut and does not know how to restore it. As an expert, you could possibly be called upon to assist. This type of maintenance activity could also be used as a training opportunity; you could show the user how to re-create the shortcut so that in future he or she would know what to do.

There will also be occasions where **upgrade** maintenance is required. When almost any aspect of a system changes, this will have an impact on the other users. It may just be a simple matter of informing them that their screen will look slightly different, or it could be that some changes will need to be made to their computer equipment for them to be able to use the system effectively. But most importantly, *they need to be informed*. You will find that, although people are frequently resistant to change, they will cooperate if you keep them informed and aware of the impact it will have.

Managing change

It is incumbent upon the IT professional practitioner to keep abreast of changes in the field, and to be able to evaluate new developments and their relevance to the working environment. There is an imperative for people within the information technology field to be aware of innovation and change.

Any improvements to the system, or the way the system is used, need to be carefully planned. There needs to be consultation with all the relevant parties throughout the process to ensure that the impact of such change is universally beneficial.

You will need to keep up to date with any new regulations and legislation and the impact that these might have on the current systems. There have been a number of new developments, particularly the Regulation of Investigatory Powers Act (2000), the revised Data Protection Act (1998) and the Human Rights Act (1998) and the many issues to do with access to data, disclosure of data and monitoring of IT activity.

Probably the most critical part of change management is the provision of appropriate and timely training and support. You need to make sure that everyone who is affected by the change is aware of it and is provided with the skills and knowledge to make it work effectively.

User support checklist

Areas supported	
hardware	
software	
other resources	
Staff supported	
colleagues	
others	
Type of support provided	
user guides	
informal training	
formal training	
ad-hoc requests	
Online support	
e-mail	
FAQ (frequently asked questions)	

Information about the company Autoware has been included in the form of a case study on pp. 157–62. It describes the nature and structure of the organisation and will provide you with a context in which to carry out this task. It is therefore essential that you read this before you attempt this activity.

Autoware uses the same calendar system that you have been studying. The company has been using it in a rather 'ad-hoc' way, that is, those who are interested use it and others don't. It has been decided by Gillian Bates, the Chief Executive, that this facility will make a considerable difference to the smooth running of the company and therefore everyone should become familiar with using it.

1. Carry out an investigation into the range of features of the software and how it might be used. Produce a report for Gillian Bates, explaining all the features and what they can be used for.

2. As it is intended to start using this software immediately, it will not be possible to provide training sessions quickly enough. You therefore need to produce a simple user guide for all the staff describing how to use the main, most frequently used aspects of the software.

Unit 308 Develop Your Own Effectiveness and Professionalism

This unit contains three elements:

308.1 Develop yourself to improve your performance
308.2 Establish and maintain effective working relationships with colleagues
308.3 Develop your own professionalism.

You need to demonstrate that you can review your own performance and identify development opportunities to improve this. You will need to show how you can establish and maintain working relationships with colleagues and line managers, communicating effectively both orally and in writing. You will need to demonstrate that you can adopt a professional attitude, exercising impartiality when assigning work, giving advice and making recommendations. You will also need to demonstrate that you can handle confidential information securely and appropriately.

To meet the requirements of this unit you should have a good understanding of the skills and abilities relevant to your responsibilities and the sources of information available to update your knowledge of IT developments. You will need to understand the overall structure of the organisation and more particularly your role in relation to immediate colleagues, to colleagues with related work activities and to line managers. You will also need to fully appreciate the importance of working relationships in maintaining the overall effectiveness of the workplace. You will need to have a good understanding of the measures available to ensure security and confidentiality of information.

Personal development

Keeping up to date

One of the most demanding aspects of working in an information technology environment is that it is always changing. Even outside of the changes that take place within an organisation which may give rise to new systems, the hardware and software are constantly developing. For example, a new, faster, better quality printer will require a new set of printer drivers, and a new version of the word processing software with additional features will need to be learned.

Whilst there will be occasions where you can reasonably expect your employer to support you in this process, you need to make sure that you do whatever you can to keep abreast of the developments in your field of expertise.

Identifying skills and knowledge

To be able to plan your skills and knowledge development, you need to know what skills you have, what skills are required and what skills you might like to have for the future.

It is a good idea to carry out a current skills analysis, that is the skills you already have. This needs to focus on a number of key areas:

- IT skills – the software you can use, the hardware you can set up, the resources you have experience of working with.
- Interpersonal skills – your people skills. How you relate to them, communicate with them and interact with them.
- Organisational skills – this is about your ability to plan the way you work and to manage yourself, your resources and others.

You need to make sure that you have all the skills that are required for you to do your job.

- There will be skills that need to be updated.
- There will be skills that need to be acquired.

And finally you need to look to the future.

- What skills and knowledge might you need as the job develops?
- What skills do you need to acquire to progress beyond your current job?

CHECK IT YOURSELF

Draw up a self-development plan. Start by carrying out a current skills analysis under the three headings listed in the text. Now look critically at your job description and, if available, a person specification. Do you have all the skills required for the job? If not, what training do you need to give you these skills? And finally, what skills and knowledge do you need for the job that your line manager does? How could you start to achieve some of these.

By going through this process you should be able to produce a self-development plan. Discuss this with your line manager, and place a copy in your portfolio as supplementary evidence.

Organisational structure

The structure of an organisation defines the lines of authority, responsibility and how control is exercised. It defines where particular activities take place and the lines of reporting. In many instances employees are not fully aware of the structure of the organisation they work in, but only of the part in which they work. However, many computer systems operate across an organisation, with each section or department having access to the relevant elements. This means that anyone who is working within the information technology environment needs to have a much greater awareness of the whole of the organisation.

Information that is supplied by one department, the primary user, may also be of value to another. For example, the sales department will be recording and processing orders from customers. It will be the primary user of this information, but the finance department will also use it to process the invoices. It is also likely that the marketing department, whilst not using the individual, detailed information about each order, will need to use summary data about orders and customers.

It is clear from this that the information, and the people who use it, do not always belong to a specific department. It is therefore extremely important that, as an expert IT user, you have a good understanding of the structure of the whole organisation in which you work. The structure of an organisation can be represented using a chart. In a large organisation it may be necessary to have one to show the overall structure, with individual charts for each department or section.

This structure may consist of a number of tiers of management, and is known as a hierarchy structure. However, in some organisations there may only be one layer of management, and the structure is then described as flat. The case study for Autoware (pp. 157–62) includes the organisation charts to describe the company.

CHECK IT YOURSELF

What is the structure of the organisation where you work? You may be able to get a copy of an organisation chart from your line manager, but it may not be up to date or even exist. Create an up-to-date structure diagram. You may need to discuss this with your line manager to make sure that you have fully understood it. Place a copy in your evidence folder as this is useful supplementary evidence.

As the information in a computer system may be being used by various different parts of the organisation, it is also extremely important to have a good understanding about this 'flow of information'. As a user of this information, you will have a better appreciation of the value of it if you know its source – where it originally came from, and who else is going to need to use it and for what purpose. This is often represented using an information flow diagram. The case study for Autoware includes an information flow diagram (p. 161).

<table>
<tr><td>

CHECK IT YOURSELF

Find out about the flow of information in your organisation and, particularly if it is a large and complex organisation, focus on the areas that you work in. In discussion with your line manager, produce an information flow diagram. Place a copy in your evidence folder as this is useful supplementary evidence.

</td></tr>
</table>

Working with people

In almost every job, there will be a requirement for you to work with other people. You may be expected to work directly or indirectly with your customers, but you will also need to work with your colleagues and managers. The key to successful working relationships is, for the most part, to be found in appropriate and thoughtful communication. The type of organisation that you work for will influence the nature of these communications. The more hierarchical the structure, the more likely the expectation of formality, but even in less formal structures there will always be instances where formal records will be necessary.

Immediate colleagues

You will need to be able to communicate with your colleagues in a number of different ways, in a variety of circumstances, and the method and styles that you use will vary to suit the situation. You will need to discuss, clarify and confirm the requirements of activities that you both undertake.

- If you are experiencing difficulties, you may need to seek assistance from colleagues. This may be in the form of information or advice, or you may need help to do some of the tasks in order to meet a deadline. It may be that you just need to alert colleagues to delays that may affect their work.
- Your colleagues may need to seek similar forms of assistance from you.
- You will need to provide information, support and possible training to support the information technology. This will be particularly important where changes are being proposed and then implemented.

Other colleagues

There may be people outside of your immediate work group with whom you need to communicate. The style of communication will tend to be more formal as the day-to-day working relationship is more distant.

- There will be occasions when someone in another department requires the product of your work. This means that he or she needs to be aware of any issues around its production and particularly about possible delays.
- There are also likely to be situations where colleagues in another department are carrying out a similar activity, and it can be extremely productive for both parties to share information and experiences.
- As previously highlighted, the very nature of organisation-wide computer systems means that changes that you might initiate may have an impact on others outside of the department, and vice versa.

Line manager

Whatever the structure of the organisation, there will be at least one person to whom you are accountable. It is essential that, regardless of personal issues, you are able to communicate effectively with your line manager. It is always a bonus if you get on with your manager, and you may need to identify an appropriate strategy to be able to complete your work to both your satisfaction. There are a number of key areas where you need to make sure you communicate with your manager.

- You should alert him or her to any possible delays in timescales. This should relate to any activities where you are responsible and should include information about reasons for the delay, possible solutions and whom else you have informed.
- You need to identify any training or support needs where this is your responsibility. These may well have arisen through changes recommended by you, or initiated by others.
- There may be improvements and changes that you would like to recommend. It is almost always a good idea to discuss these, albeit informally, with your line manager before turning it into a formal proposal.
- There will probably be formal summary reports that you are required to make, for example, details of IT training provided in the department in the last six months. It is important that these are presented in the required format and on time.
- You should also identify the training, support, etc., that you need. Your manager will want to know how you propose to maintain and increase your expertise, but remember to present it as a development plan that includes your input as well as your expectations from the organisation.

Professionalism

A professional is someone who works within a recognised set of standards, with an expectation of commitment to performing competently. At this level, it is essential that you operate in a professional way.

Confidentiality of information

Almost all organisations have information that they wish to be treated as confidential. There will be many different reasons why information is to be considered confidential. Some aspects of confidentiality of data are covered by legislation, for example data covered under the Data Protection Act (see page 9) – remember almost all personal data held in an organised form is covered by this legislation. This information may be about employees, clients, and customers; it is all covered by the legislation.

There will also be other information that needs to be handled confidentially.

- There may be information that is available to you, as part of the tasks you are expected to carry out, which should not be made available to your colleagues. For example, you may take part in discussions about planned changes to the computer system that will have an impact on the way people work. Whilst it may eventually be your role to support staff in these changes, it will often be the case that during the early planning stages, when the full impact has not been finalised, that this information is not for general dissemination. It would also, usually, be the responsibility of the manager to inform staff of these changes.
- There may be business information that you handle which should be kept confidential from the organisation's customers. For example, the designs for a new product, particularly in the early stages, will need to be confidential so as to reduce the risk of a competitor taking advantage of this information.

Impartiality

Part of being a professional is about making informed judgements. It is essential that these judgements are made fairly, and are seen to be fair.

- There may be occasions when you will need to make judgements about people's work-loads. You may be responsible for assigning work to individuals. There are always certain jobs that people like to do, perhaps because they are personally satisfying or maybe because they do not involve working late. It is important that the distribution of these types of jobs is decided on a fair basis. It could be reasonably argued that staff who are carers after work should not usually be given work that may result in them having to work late, or that everyone with the necessary skills has an opportunity to do the 'fun' job. Likewise, it is necessary to make sure that it is not always the same person who ends up working late.

- When you are required to give advice, support or training for your colleagues, you need to be certain that this advice is impartial. In a situation where one person may be more dependent upon you than others it may be difficult not to appear to be favouring the individual and you will need to make sure that your expertise is made available fairly.

- Recommendations need to be based on facts. You might be making recommendations about the training needs of others, a change to the system or suggesting a change in the software, hardware or materials that are used. It must be clear that these recommendations are designed to improve the functioning of the department and therefore provide an improvement for the organisation.

Within own competence

Within your current job role, you will be expected to have the skills and knowledge necessary to carry out the main activities competently. It is important that you can identify your own levels of competence.

- There will inevitably be, particularly in a field that is subject to so much change, tasks which you are not yet able to perform. It is essential that you recognise and acknowledge these limitations, alerting others to the need for this work to be carried out by others and also identifying scope for further self-development and training needs.

- You may be called upon to support your colleagues; do not attempt to provide this assistance if you are not fully competent yourself as this could easily give rise to further confusion.

OPTIONAL UNITS

Unit 305 Design and Produce Documents Using Word Processing Software

This unit contains four elements:

305.1 Design the layout and presentation of documents
305.2 Create the required documents
305.3 Contribute to improving design and production
305.4 Output document to the required destination.

You need to demonstrate that you can interpret your customer's requirements to design document layouts taking into account the facilities and constraints of the available resources. You will need to demonstrate that you are competent in producing a variety of complex word processing documents, using facilities to format, manipulate, structure and establish dynamic links where applicable for the required documents. You will also need to demonstrate that you can identify opportunities to improve the design and production of documents, presenting your recommendations to the relevant person. You will need to show that you can correctly identify appropriate output devices and output parameters to produce the required documents.

To meet the requirements of this unit, you should have a good understanding of the importance of thoroughly investigating the customer's requirements and of being able to work within imposed constraints. You will need to know a wide range of facilities within the word processing software and the factors affecting the choice of facilities and functions to meet the requirements for the documents. You will need to fully appreciate the facilities available for automation of formatting and how these can enhance the effective production of documents. You will also need to understand the importance of making clear your recommendations to the relevant person, and being receptive to views of colleagues. You should have a good understanding of the factors affecting your choice of output device and the importance of ensuring confidentiality of the information.

Introduction

Word processing is the term used to describe general-purpose software designed to support and enhance computer-based production of primarily text-based documents. In most organisations, letters and internal communications such as memos, forms and reports are prepared using word processing software. Modern word processing facilities have features way beyond those that would have previously been carried out using a typewriter. Many documents are now produced in-house that would previously have been sent out for professional production by a printer, or may have been created using specialist software such as desktop publishing (DTP).

The printed document is one of the ways that an organisation presents itself to the outside world and, internally, to its shareholders, managers and staff. It is therefore extremely important that due consideration is given to the appearance of any document. Most organisations will usually have very clearly defined rules, a **house style**, within which they require all staff to produce documents. This house style will precisely define the use of the name of the organisation, any logos, trade marks, etc., and what must and must not be done with them. The size and type of font used will usually be specified for external communications, and there may well be rules about page numbering, style of date and much more. For internal communications, these rules may be a little more relaxed, although the structure of memos may be defined, style of numbering systems to be used in formal reports and author referencing systems required will often still be specified.

CHECK IT YOURSELF

The house style checklist on p. 86 includes all the main house style features you need to be aware of for the standard documents in your organisation. As you progress through the qualification, complete the checklist so that you can include this in your evidence folder as supplementary evidence.

Specification

The specification for a word processing document can take many forms. Documents that are largely text-based will usually only require details about fonts, paragraph styles, page layout, etc., whilst those containing other types of data, such as tables, images, colour or data from linked sources, will need much greater detail.

The specification will need to identify the following:

- The purpose – what the document is going to be used for, eg letter, report, internal communication.
- The audience – who is going to receive it? Are they from within the organisation or external? Are they senior members of the organisation?
- The structure of the document – sections, numbering, etc.
- The image to be projected – what is the tone to be set, is humour appropriate? Should there be an emphasis on facts and figures or is this about raising awareness and encouraging discussion?
- The content – this may include the exact text, the images to be used, colour schemes required, etc., or it may offer you varying levels of design flexibility.
- The media – is the finished product to be provided on paper, letter-headed stationery, specialist stationery, or on disk or to be e-mailed?
- The hardware and software available – what platform is it to be developed and delivered on? What version of the software is available? Are colour prints required?

CHECK IT YOURSELF

You will need to find out all this information from your client. Sometimes it may be provided in a clear and precise way, but often it will not. As it is important that any documents you produce meet the requirements of your client, it would be useful for you to design an easy-to-use specification sheet that could help during the process.

Design

Page layout

One of the first considerations when designing a document will be regarding the layout of the whole page. You will need to take into account the requirements of your client but also the constraints and limitations that may be imposed by the available software and printing facilities.

- Page size
  If you are using a laser printer or ink jet printer it will usually be A4 (210×297 mm or 8.27×11.69 in) although you may also use Legal (8.5×14 in) or Letter (8.5×11 in). Some printers may also be able to handle A3 or even A5 paper. Most printers are also capable of handling various specialist stationery, such as envelopes and labels.

- Orientation

  You will need to decide the orientation of the pages, portrait or landscape. Sometimes it may be necessary for different sections of the same document to have a different page orientation.

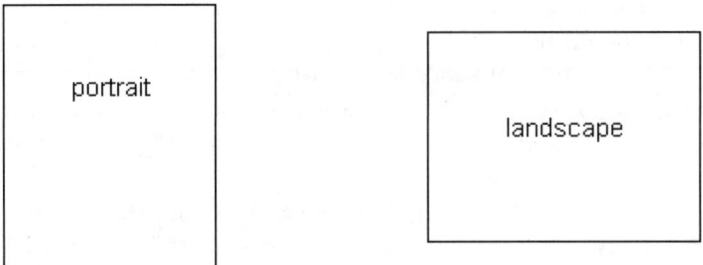

Figure 15 *Paper orientation*

- Margins

  The usable area on the page in which you can place the main part of your document is controlled by setting the size of the four margins – top, bottom, left and right. These may also be varied for different sections of the same document.

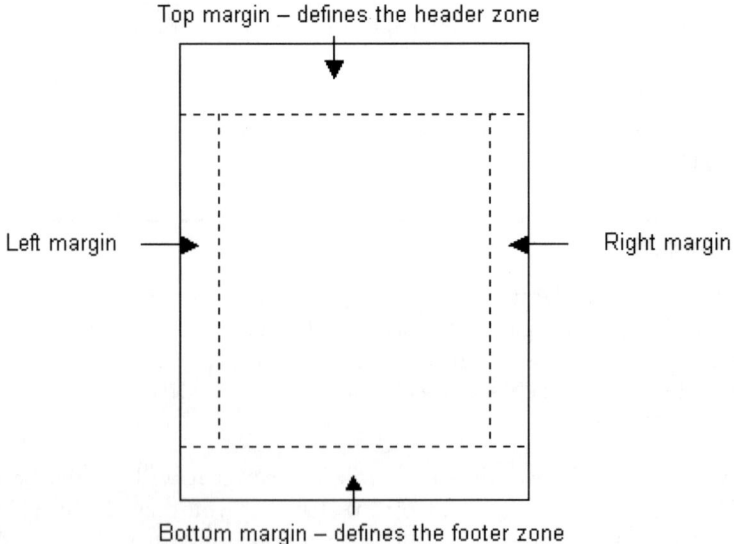

Figure 16 *Page margins*

- Headers and footers

  A header is text that appears in the header zone defined by the top margin and it appears at the top of every page. A footer is text that appears in the footer zone defined by the bottom margin and it appears at the bottom of every page. Headers and footers can be set up so that they are different for odd and even pages of a document, or different on the first page of a document. Headers and footers can also be varied for different sections of the document. Headers and footers are frequently used for page numbering, document references and dates.

- Page numbering

  The software will usually let you specify whether you want the pages of a document to be numbered automatically and where these should appear, in the header or the footer. You will also be able to include such controls as omitting the number on page 1, something you often want to do particularly with letters, or starting the numbering from any number. This is useful where the document is only part of the final product.

- Columns

  You may need to organise the content of your document into columns. These columns could be newspaper style, where the text flows to the bottom of the first column and then starts again at the top of the next, or parallel columns, where each discrete section of text starts at the same line in the column next to it. You will need to use different features of the software to achieve these two types of presentation.

Paragraph layout

- Justification

  The justification of the text in a paragraph defines how the text is aligned within the margins. This can be left, right, centre or full.

This is an example of *left*-justified text. The left margin is aligned but the right margin is ragged.	This is an example of *right*-justified text. The right margin is aligned but the left margin is ragged.	This is an example of *centre*-justified text. The text is aligned to the centre of the page and the left and right margins are ragged.	This is an example of text that has *full* justification. Both the left and right margins are aligned. It is achieved by the software spreading the text to fit the margins by inserting additional *soft* spaces.

Figure 17 *Types of justification*

- Indentation

  A paragraph may be indented at the left, right or both margins. The left hand margin of the first line of each paragraph may be indented, or a paragraph may have a hanging indent, that is second and all subsequent lines are set in on the left margin by a specified amount.

CHECK IT YOURSELF

The word processing checklist on p. 88 includes all the main layout features you need to be able to use in your particular software. As you progress through the qualification, complete section 1 so that you can include this in your evidence folder as supplementary evidence.

- Line spacing

  The spacing between the lines of text is a very important presentation feature in any document. In most types of documents it is usual to have an additional line space between each paragraph. Until recently this was most frequently achieved by putting an additional hard return in the document. However, it is now considered better to control the amount of space above and/or below each paragraph by setting this in the paragraph format facility. You can also change the line spacing between the lines of text within the paragraph by adjusting the line spacing. In many word processing packages this will include single, double and 1.5 line spacing; double line spacing is often used for printing a draft of a document so that there is sufficient space for amendments to be written on the document.

- Tabs

  Tabulation is available to help you align columns of information within a paragraph. You can do this by placing *tabs* in the required positions on a ruler. These tabs can be set for left, right, centre or decimal alignment, depending on the type of data to be included.

- Number lists

  There are many occasions when a document will contain a list of items or indeed a sequence of paragraphs. Sometimes these lists will need to have some form of numbering system attached to indicate their sequence. The most effective way of achieving this is to use the automatic numbering feature available in the software. This will then enable the numbers to be updated automatically if you need to add or delete items or paragraphs.

- Bullets

  Sometimes the list of items included in a document should not be numbered as the items do not have any specific order attached to them.

Each item in the list can be started with a 'bullet', which can be one of the standard symbols available or can be defined by the user.

- Tables

  There are many occasions when the data to be included in a word processing document needs to be presented as a table. Your word processing software will have the tools to enable you to do this. You will need to identify the number of columns and rows required, although these can usually be altered quite easily. Each intersection of a column and row is known as a cell. Each cell can contain an item of data, text or numbers. The alignment of the data in the cells can be controlled in the same way as other paragraphs, that is left, centre, right or full. Within a cell the data is organised into paragraphs and therefore the wordwrap facilities will cause text that does not fit to move down to the next line, adjusting the depth of the row to accommodate it.

  The table can be displayed with or without grid lines, and you can use a range of line and shading or colour facilities to enhance its presentation.

CHECK IT YOURSELF

The word processing checklist on p. 88 includes all the main presentation features you need to be able to use in your particular software. As you progress through the qualification, complete section 2 so that you can include this in your evidence folder as supplementary evidence.

Text format

The way the text looks, the ease with which it can be read and the overall visual effect are also important and need to be included in the specification. It is rarely advisable for a document to consist of too many different effects as the impact of the different appearances may get in the way of the content.

- Font

  The shape and style of the text can be varied enormously. Most printers will support a considerable number of different fonts. Some are very plain and clear and therefore more appropriate for business applications, whilst others are much more fancy and elaborate and are very effective for less formal communications or possibly for posters and leaflets.

- Size

  Not only can you use different fonts, but you can also control the size. With printers capable of producing very high-quality print, it is not only possible to print very small, fine characters quite clearly but also to print very large letters. Most fonts are measured in points – the higher the number, the larger the character.

- Borders and shading

    A paragraph, group of paragraphs or a page can be separated from the rest of the text with the appropriate use of borders, lines and shading. There will be a range of features available within your package and these can be used to considerably enhance the overall presentation of the document.

CHECK IT YOURSELF

The word processing checklist on p. 88 includes all the main format features you need to be able to use in your particular software. As you progress through the qualification, complete section 3 so that you can include this in your evidence folder as supplementary evidence.

Production

Manipulation of text

In order to achieve the requirements of your clients and take full advantage of the capabilities of the software, you will need to know how to use the text manipulation facilities of the word processing software. You will need to be able to use the copy, move (cut and paste), insert, delete and the search and replace commands with confidence.

There will be times when information contained within one document needs to be included in another. In these cases, the insert file facility makes a copy of the original document and transfers it to the one you are working on. This can be extremely useful, for example if a number of people are involved in the production of a large document, each one can work in a separate file which can be merged together into one file when completed, or where a standard piece of text may need to be included in a number of different documents.

You may also wish to insert data from another application, for example an extract from a spreadsheet or database file. When you insert data from another application it is possible for this file to be dynamically linked, this means that when the data changes in the original file the linked file will also be updated. This, of course, is not what you always want. Quite often you want to have a 'snap-shot' of the data at a particular moment in time. The simplest way to achieve this is to use the copy and paste facilities of your software application, placing the data on the 'clip-board' to transfer between the two applications. When using this method, the data from a spreadsheet or database will usually be inserted into the word processing document as a table.

For data within a table, there may be occasions when you will need to reorganise the order in which the rows of data are presented. This is a relatively straightforward function, but it is one that should be carried out with great care. As with any significant amendment to a document, it is always sensible to save your work before manipulating it in this way.

Manipulation of graphics

Many documents produced using a word processing package will require the inclusion of some form of graphical image. The images may come from a variety of sources and will be in a very wide range of formats. Most word processing software is capable of handling the more commonly used formats without any manipulation, whilst other formats may still require the use of some graphics software to convert to appropriate file type.

Image	File extension
Graphics interchange format	gif
Tag image file format	tif
Windows meta file	wmf
Targa	tga
Windows bitmap	bmp
Windows paintbrush	pcx
Encapsulated postscript	eps
JPEG	jpg
MPEG	mpg
Drawing exchange file	dxf
Photo cd	pcd

Many of the images you need to use will already exist in electronic form; there is an ever-growing bank of 'clip-art' available, and most organisations have images such as the company logo available in electronic form. Other images will exist, but only in paper form. You will need to use a scanner with appropriate image-capture and manipulation software to convert them to digital form for use in your document. Using a scanner is a relatively straightforward process, but it is recommended that you spend the time at image-capture stage ensuring that the image is correct, as this will save considerable time later when producing the document.

The graphics will usually only form part of the document. You will need to be able to insert them in appropriate places, and then manipulate them to fit in with the overall requirements of the document. This may mean altering the size of the image without distorting it; that is maintaining the *aspect ratio*. The text flow will need to be controlled; the text may need to flow around the image, behind the image or after the image.

CHECK IT YOURSELF

The word processing checklist on p. 88 includes all the main document manipulation features you need to be able to use in your particular software. As you progress through the qualification, complete section 4 so that you can include this in your evidence folder as supplementary evidence.

Arithmetic

When working with data in a table, you should be able to carry out some basic arithmetic. This is achieved by placing a formula in the cell of the table that is to contain the answer. This formula will refer to the cells that contain the values to be used in the calculation. You can also use absolute values within your formula to provide a value that is not within the cells of the table, for example you could calculate the VAT based on a value in a cell by multiplying the cell by 17.5%. The basic arithmetic operators (+, −, * and /) are used and there may be some basic functions available, for example the SUM function can be used to add up all the values in a row or a column; the AVERAGE function calculates the arithmetic mean of a row or a column.

CHECK IT YOURSELF

The word processing checklist on p. 89 includes all the main arithmetic features you need to be able to use in your particular software. As you progress through the qualification, complete section 5 so that you can include this in your evidence folder as supplementary evidence.

Structure

- Captions and cross-referencing

    A caption is a numbered label, such as "Figure 1", that you can add to a table, figure, equation, or other item. You will be able to specify where the caption appears in relation to the object it relates to. A cross-reference is a reference to an item that appears in another location in a document, for example, "See Figure 1 on page 3". You can create cross-references to headings, footnotes, bookmarks, captions, numbered paragraphs, and so on. If you later add, delete, or move an item you have referred to in a cross-reference, you can easily generate a revised cross-reference.

- Table of contents

    A table of contents lists, in page number order, the contents of a document. It will usually appear at the start of the document and will be based on the headings and sub-headings in the document. By using the table of contents facilities of the word processing software, when amendments are made to any part of the document the table can be re-generated.

- Indexing

    An index is another means of referencing the contents of a document. However, an index is based on identified key words and is displayed in alphabetical order, identifying the page or pages where it appears, and is usually included at the end of the document. Each key word to be included in the index is tagged and then the index is generated. When changes are made to the document, the index can be re-generated to reflect these amendments.

CHECK IT YOURSELF

The word processing checklist on p. 89 includes all the main structure definition features you need to be able to use in your particular software. As you progress through the qualification, complete section 6 so that you can include this in your evidence folder as supplementary evidence.

Automated formatting

- Macros

    There are some tasks in word processing that you carry out frequently and, to save time, you can create a macro to do this task. Macro is the name given to a set of simple instructions that can be used to perform a repetitive task. In most word processing packages you can *record* the tasks as a macro and then make modifications to it afterwards to enhance and extend it if necessary.

- Styles

  In most word processing systems you can define paragraph styles. These define the features of the paragraph, including the font, size, line spacing, tabs, lines and borders and language. The use of styles makes it easier to ensure consistency throughout a document. If you need to change any aspect of the paragraph, you can modify the style definition and apply it throughout the document.

- Paragraph style

  A paragraph is defined by the text between two hard returns. To ensure consistency of presentation and to assist in re-designing a document, you can define the different styles that you need in a document. By giving each style a unique name, you can specify the paragraph styles required and only need to modify this definition in order to make the changes throughout the document.

- Templates

  A template is a ready to use, document definition. It can be set up to define the layout, fonts, styles and settings for a document. You can also include standard text such as the letter-head information including the company logo, header and/or footer text and page numbering.

- Mail merge

  Mail merge is a facility, available in most word processors, that lets you merge a text-based document with sets of data to produce individual documents. You could use mail merge to produce the same letter to all your customers, but with each letter individually addressed. You can mail merge a word processing document with an existing data file created in the word processing software or *imported* from a spreadsheet or a database. You can also create a new data file using the word processing software. There will usually be some form of 'helper' or 'wizard' to assist in this process.

CHECK IT YOURSELF

The word processing checklist on p. 89 includes all the main automated formatting features you need to be able to use in your particular software. As you progress through the qualification, complete section 7 so that you can include this in your evidence folder as supplementary evidence.

Hard copy

For all the applications software that you use, you will need to know the output capabilities of the package. You will need to know all the parameters that need to be provided and how they operate with the particular equipment you are using. Modern laser printers are capable of carrying out many activities over and above simple printing (see p. 36).

You will need to make sure that you know how to control the output of your documents from the word processing software. This will include double-sided printing, printing a specific page or range of pages, orientation of the page, and printing on different sizes and types of stationery. You may also be able to control the collation of multiple copies, including sorting and stapling.

House style checklist

Section 1: letters	
paper size	
logo	
position of date	
reference	
position of addressee details	
font	
type size	
justification	
margins	
line spacing	
page numbering	
Section 2: memos	
paper size	
logo	
position of date	
reference	
position of addressee details	
font	
type size	
justification	
margins	
line spacing	
page numbering	
Section 3: internal reports	
paper size	
logo	
position of date	
reference	
position of addressee details	
font	

House style checklist (continued)

type size	
justification	
margins	
line spacing	
page numbering	
Section 4: external reports	
paper size	
logo	
position of date	
reference	
position of addressee details	
font	
type size	
justification	
margins	
line spacing	
page numbering	

Word processing checklist

Section 1: layout features	
page size	
orientation	
margins	
headers and footers	
page numbering	
columns	
paragraph justification	
paragraph indentation	
Section 2: presentation features	
line spacing	
tabs	
numbered lists	
bulleted lists	
tables	
Section 3: format features	
text – font	
size	
emphasis	
colour	
borders	
shading	
Section 4: documentation manipulation	
copy	
move (cut and paste)	
insert	
delete	
search and replace	
sort	
graphics	

Word processing checklist (continued)

Section 5: arithmetic features	
basic arithmetic (+, −, *, /)	
sum function	
average function	
Section 6: structure definition	
captions	
cross-referencing	
table of contents	
index	
Section 7: automated formatting features	
macros	
styles	
paragraph styles	
templates	
mail merge	

Case Study Activity

Information about the company Autoware has been included in the form of a case study on pp. 157–62. It describes the nature and structure of the organisation and will provide you with a context in which to carry out this task. It is therefore essential that you read this before you attempt this activity.

Like many other modern businesses, Autoware have decided that it needs to update its image. The company believes that this is necessary not only to retain their current customers but also to expand.

As part of this process it has been recognised that the company house style needs to be reviewed. Although the majority of its communication is electronic within the organisation, the Chief Executive, Gillian Bates, still requires that all document types are included.

1. This 're-branding' of an organisation has been a frequently occurring event in recent years. Carry out some research into how other organisations have gone about this, with particular reference to the adoption of a new, 'modern' house style. The Internet will be a good source for some of this information.

2. You now need to create a house style guide for the following types of documents:

    -   letters
    -   memos
    -   internal e-mails
    -   external e-mails
    -   internal reports
    -   external reports.

    You will need to include all the required elements of each of these documents, including details of templates, graphics and other electronic resources and where they are located.

Unit 306 Design and Produce Spreadsheets

This unit contains four elements:

306.1 Design the layout and presentation of spreadsheets
306.2 Create the required spreadsheet
306.3 Produce graphical representation of numerical information
306.4 Output spreadsheet to the required destination.

You need to demonstrate that you can interpret your customer's requirements to design spreadsheet layouts taking into account the facilities and constraints of the available resources. You will need to demonstrate that you are competent in producing a variety of complex spreadsheet documents, using facilities to format, manipulate, calculate and to establish dynamic links where applicable for the required documents. You will need to demonstrate that you can use the software to produce graphical representations of numerical information. You will also need to show that you can correctly identify appropriate output devices and output parameters to produce the required documents.

To meet the requirements of this unit you should have a good understanding of the importance of thoroughly investigating the customer's requirements and of being able to work within imposed constraints. You will need to know a wide range of facilities within the spreadsheet software and the factors affecting the choice of facilities and functions to meet the requirements for the documents. You will need to fully understand the factors affecting choice of graphical representation type and the importance of effective annotation of the graph. You should have a good understanding of the factors affecting your choice of output device and the importance of ensuring confidentiality of the information.

Introduction

Spreadsheets provide a very versatile and flexible tool. They are designed to provide the user with an easy-to-use package, primarily for the manipulation of numerical data. There are many different ways to use them and they are suitable for all kinds of different applications. Typically, they are used to support financial applications, for statistical analysis and to assist with data modelling. A spreadsheet package will also provide you with facilities to represent the data graphically in the form of charts and graphs.

A spreadsheet is like a very large, electronic piece of paper which is arranged in rows and columns. The intersection of each row and column is called a cell and is referenced using its *column* letter and *row* number, eg **D4**.

A cell can contain one item of data which can be one of the following:

- Text – any character. This data type is generally used for headings, usually needed at the top of a column or the beginning of a row. Data of this type cannot be used in any numerical calculations.
- Numeric – real numbers, used in calculations and sometimes for other special data types, such as dates.
- Formula – to carry out calculations, usually making reference to other cells to be used in the calculations.

Calculations within a spreadsheet are usually recalculated every time data is entered into a cell, reflecting any changes made to the referenced cells. In very large spreadsheets that include many calculations and high volumes of data input, the auto-calculation may be turned off as it can cause the spreadsheet to work very slowly, with the user making a forced re-calculation when the input is complete.

Requirements specification

The design of the spreadsheet is very important. As spreadsheets can be used in so many different ways, it is necessary to clearly identify the requirements so that you can make the best use of the capabilities of the software.

The specification will need to identify the following:

- The purpose – what the spreadsheet is going to be used for, eg monthly and summary budgets.
- The data sources – where is the data going to come from and is this internal or external to the organisation?
- The data items – every item of data to be used, eg budget headings, totals.
- The characteristics of the data – data type, size and format of every item of data.
- The methods of input – eg keyboard, mouse, etc.
- The layout of the input – what does the data look like at source and what will the input screens look like?
- The processes to be carried out on the data – any calculations, selections, manipulations and does the data need to be represented graphically?
- The recipients of the information – who is going to receive the information and when?

- The layout of the output – what do the paper-based reports look like?
- The media for output – paper, disk, etc.
- The hardware and software available – what platform is it to be developed and delivered on? What version of the software is available? Are colour prints required?

Design

You may be given a design layout by your client – this might be a copy of what it looks like as it is done at the moment, or you might just have the specification you have written. You will need to create the model and it is usually a good idea to draw a few outline designs, or sketches, on a piece of paper before you try to set up the spreadsheet.

You will usually start by working out what rows and columns you need, and of course these will all need labels. In going through this stage, you will have also identified the places (cells) where the numeric data will go. Then you need to work out the formulae you will need to carry out all the calculations required.

When you are designing a spreadsheet solution, you need to consider not only the layout of the main data required for the problem but also some of the constant data that may be needed. Constant data are data items that are fixed, for example the rate of VAT. However, although they are fixed, it may be that they can change. If you need to use data of this kind, it is usually a good idea to include them in cells somewhere in the spreadsheet rather than embedded in a formula. If they are embedded in a formula, then someone who understands the formula, the syntax of the formula, and has access to the formula will need to change it, whereas if they are in cells, then the user can change them.

Another good reason to include constant data in cells rather than in formulae is that they can be included in the display of the solution. This means that when they change, it will be easier to identify that this solution is based on the new value.

The design, the formulae, or rules, together with the column and row headings define the model. Spreadsheets are often used to create a model which will then be used for many different sets of data. In this situation, you would need to save a copy of the spreadsheet which only contained the labels and the formulae, ie without any data. This model would also need to be printed showing the formulae so that the model is fully documented and can be used by others.

Layout

In addition to all the layout considerations that you will take into account to ensure that your spreadsheet will enable you to provide an accurate solution, you will need to make sure that your final product will result in a high quality document. You will need to be mindful of all the standards and conventions required by your organisation (see house styles in Unit 305 on p. 74).

Many of the layout features are the same and you will need to take all of them into account as you design and produce your spreadsheets. You will need to know how to change the orientation of the page, include headers and footers, use page numbering and date/time stamping. You will need to know how to use features such as adjusting the four margins (top, bottom, left and right), displaying or suppressing grid lines and 'best-fit' to ensure all the required information is displayed.

There are many facilities in most spreadsheet packages that enable you to further enhance the presentation of your documents. You can control the size of the display of the data, emphasise it using features such as bold, italics and underlining, and you will probably have access to a wide range of fonts. The highlighting of key items can also be improved by the appropriate use of borders, lines and shading. If the spreadsheets are going to be used frequently by viewing the screen, or if colour printing facilities are available, then the presentation can be further enhanced by judicious use of colour.

CHECK IT YOURSELF

The spreadsheet checklist on p. 105 includes all the main layout features you need to be able to use in your particular software. As you progress through the qualification, complete section 1 so that you can include this in your evidence folder as supplementary evidence.

Data formats

The default display width of a column is usually sufficient to display approximately nine characters. This will vary between packages and, where you are working with proportional spacing fonts, will depend upon the particular characters included. The width of the column only relates to the *display* of the column; you can always put more than nine characters into the cell but they may not all be displayed. The way data that cannot be fully displayed in a cell is treated depends upon what type of data it is. You need to be mindful of the impact on your design when you change the width to display all the data in a cell; as the spreadsheet structure is based around columns, you cannot change the width of a single cell but only the width of the whole column.

If the cell is not wide enough and it contains text and there is something in the cell to the right of it, the text will be *truncated* (cut short).

If the cell is not wide enough and it contains text and the cell to the right of it is *empty*, it will continue into the next cell. This is very useful for titles at the top of the sheet which are frequently much longer than the standard width of a cell.

If the cell is not wide enough and it contains numeric data it will often be displayed as a row of hash signs (########) to warn you that there is not enough room to display the number; it would be very unhelpful if numbers were truncated – you would often not notice this and the wrong results would be displayed! Sometimes the scientific notation is used; 5.98E+09 is actually 5,980,000,000.

You will need to decide exactly how the data should be displayed, that is what formats are required. The default display for text data is left aligned within the cell. Sometimes, particularly when used as column headings, it would make the spreadsheet easier to read if the text was displayed as right or centre aligned. You will usually also be able to align text data over a range of cells so that you could, for example, centre a heading across all the cells it relates to. You will also be able to increase the depth of the row and use wordwrap facilities to include longer text in one cell.

The default display for numeric data is right aligned within the cell. This is of course how numeric data should be aligned; a left or centre-aligned column of figures does not easily display the numerical significance of the numbers and is therefore not useful. However, there are a number of factors to take into account when displaying numeric data.

When all the numbers in the spreadsheet are *integers* (whole numbers) the data is displayed in an easily readable format. However, when you enter numbers that include a decimal point the default display does not include *non-significant* zeros (except the one immediately preceding the decimal point). For example:

10.00	is displayed as:	10
10.50	is displayed as:	10.5
.45	is displayed as:	0.45
00.342	is displayed as:	0.342
1.8687	is displayed as:	1.8687

As you can see, although the numbers are right aligned, they are difficult to read as they are not aligned on the decimal place. This is the default display for all numeric data and is known as *general* format. There will be a range of formats available for numeric data in your spreadsheet software which will let you define the alignment of the decimal point and the degree of precision, ie how many decimal places are required. By default, this will be achieved by rounding up or down; for example, 0.342 would be rounded down to 0.34 whereas 1.868 would be rounded up to 1.87. You will be able to include currency and percentage signs within numeric cells and also to define your own formats.

CHECK IT YOURSELF

The spreadsheet checklist on p. 105 includes all the main data formatting features you need to be able to use in your particular software. As you progress through the qualification, complete section 2 so that you can include this in your evidence folder as supplementary evidence.

Calculation facilities

The primary reason for using spreadsheets to provide an information technology solution is that they are particularly useful for carrying out calculations. Calculations are achieved by placing *formulae* or *functions* into a cell. You will need to make sure that you know how to include formulae to carry out addition, subtraction, multiplication and division.

Any formula can include reference to any cell or block of cells in the spreadsheet. These cell references may be *relative*, ie when the formula is copied the reference is adjusted relative to where it is copied, or *absolute*, ie when the formula is copied the cell reference remains unchanged. Cells, or blocks of cells, can also be given a name; this name can then be used whenever you need to reference the cell and is *absolute* in its nature. You can also include absolute values in a formula but you should bear in mind the issues discussed under Design earlier in the unit.

Cell	Formula	What it does
B15	=B7+B12	Adds the value in B7 to the value in B12 and displays the result in B15
C15	=C10–C11	Subtracts the value in C11 from the value in C10 and displays the result in C15
D15	=D13*D14	Multiplies the value in D13 by the value in D14 and displays the result in D15
E15	=E8/E9	Divides the value in E8 by the value in E9 and displays the result in E15
F15	=F3*5	Multiplies the value in F3 by the absolute value 5 and displays the result in F15
G15	=Qty*Price	Multiplies the value in the named cell Qty by the value in the named cell Price and displays the result in G15

As spreadsheets have been developed to support significant calculations, many standard, but more complex, calculations can be achieved through the use of functions. There are functions for a very wide range of types of application and you will need to use those relevant for your spreadsheet. However, you should at the very least be competent with the basic functions as follows:

Cell	Function	What it does
B15	=SUM(B7:B12)	Adds the values in the range of cells between B7 and B12 and displays the result in B15
C15	=AVERAGE(C7:C12)	Adds the values in the range of cells between C7 and C12 and divides this by the number of values in the range, ie calculates the arithmetic mean
D15	=MEDIAN(D7:D12)	Identifies the mid-point value in the range of cells between D7 and D12 and displays the result in D15
E15	=MODE(E7:E12)	Identifies the most frequently occurring value in the range of cells between E7 and E12 and displays the result in E15
F15	=MIN(F7:F12)	Identifies the lowest value in the range of cells between F7 and F12 and displays the result in F15
G15	=MAX(G7:G12)	Identifies the highest value in the range of cells between G7 and G12 and displays the result in G15
H15	=COUNT(H7:H12)	Counts how many values there are in the range of cells between H7 and H12 and displays the result in H15

Worksheet manipulation

In order to achieve the requirements of your clients and take full advantage of the capabilities of the software, you will need to know how to use the text manipulation facilities of the spreadsheet software. You will need to be able to use the copy, paste, move, insert and delete commands with confidence.

There may be occasions when you will need to reorganise the order in which the rows of data are presented. Although this is a relatively straightforward function, it is one that should be carried out with great care as it is possible to destroy completely the validity of the data in the sheet. It is therefore always sensible to save your work before manipulating it in this way.

The most likely error that will occur is that you will sort the data in the specified column and the data in the other columns will remain where they were. For example:

Before the sort

TRAVEL EXPENSES FOR SALES DEPARTMENT STAFF							
Name		**January**	**February**	**March**	**April**	**May**	**June**
Kerry	Walker	117.50	106.25	89.45	113.00	98.67	89.79
Julian	Peters	45.67	34.67	87.56	56.78	45.56	34.69
Adrian	Walsh	54.76	56.00	60.20	45.90	34.50	45.67
Gillian	Armstrong	23.34	24.50	26.40	21.34	22.98	25.00
Bella	Epong	39.00	38.00	37.00	38.00	39.00	40.00
Tushar	Patel	12.19	14.60	18.96	18.75	18.75	21.07

After the sort – can you identify the error?

TRAVEL EXPENSES FOR SALES DEPARTMENT STAFF							
Name		January	February	March	April	May	June
Gillian	Armstrong	117.50	106.25	89.45	113.00	98.67	89.79
Bella	Epong	45.67	34.67	87.56	56.78	45.56	34.69
Tushar	Patel	54.76	56.00	60.20	45.90	34.50	45.67
Julian	Peters	23.34	24.50	26.40	21.34	22.98	25.00
Kerry	Walker	39.00	38.00	37.00	38.00	39.00	40.00
Adrian	Walsh	12.19	14.60	18.96	18.75	18.75	21.07

CHECK IT YOURSELF

The spreadsheet checklist on p. 106 includes all the main data manipulation features you need to be able to use in your particular software. As you progress through the qualification, complete section 4 so that you can include this in your evidence folder as supplementary evidence.

Links

Sometimes, in a manual situation, the solution to a problem does not fit neatly on to one piece of paper. It is therefore not surprising that, at times, you need to come up with a multi-sheet solution. The spreadsheet you are working with will undoubtedly have the facilities to have more than one sheet in a spreadsheet file. This means that you can organise the layout of your solution to use a number of spreadsheets, and the data can be referenced between the sheets.

There are also times when you might need to bring together the data from several separate spreadsheet files. Again, the software you are working with will have the facilities to take data from one spreadsheet file and include it in another. These links are usually dynamic, that is when the data is changed in the sheet, these changes are automatically reflected in the linked sheet.

It is also possible to use the data from a spreadsheet in another application. The most common application of this type is in a word processing solution. When you dynamically copy the data from a spreadsheet to a word processing package it will usually be displayed in the form of a table. As this link is dynamic, any changes to the original spreadsheet data will automatically be reflected in the word processing document. You can also transfer data from your spreadsheet to another application without these links. There will be occasions when you require a 'snap-shot' of the data. You can achieve this by using the copy and paste features of your environment, placing the data on the clip-board, to make it available in your other application.

You may also need to *export* the data into a format that can be used by a range of applications. Spreadsheet data can be exported in a *comma delimited* format. The resulting file will contain each data item from each row of the spreadsheet, separated by commas. Each new row will start on a new line, that is there will be a carriage return code included in the file. Where there is an empty cell, one comma will be immediately followed by another. This format may also be referred to as **csv** format (see Figure 18). This format is recognised by many different applications packages and is the industry standard for exporting data of this kind.

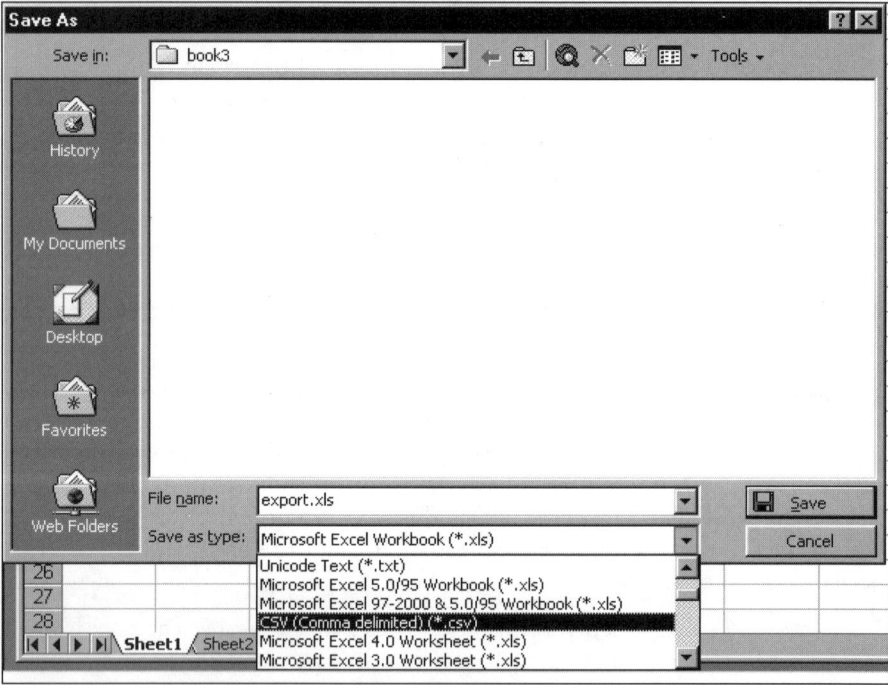

Figure 18 *CSV format*

CHECK IT YOURSELF

The spreadsheet checklist on p. 106 includes all the main link facilities you need to be able to use in your particular software. As you progress through the qualification, complete section 5 so that you can include this in your evidence folder as supplementary evidence.

Spreadsheet graphics

Spreadsheet software is usually used because it is particularly good at handling numeric data and, whilst in many instances the actual values need to be displayed, there are many occasions when graphical representation of this data can make the meaning clearer and easier to understand. Spreadsheet packages will usually have charting capabilities and tools such as wizards to aid in their production.

It is extremely important that an appropriate graph type is used; these software tools will run on any data that you provide, and this means that it is possible to produce an invalid and meaningless graph.

Bar (column) chart

A bar chart is used to display the *frequencies* of a set of data. It is drawn with either vertical or horizontal bars of comparative lengths. Bar charts are particularly suitable if you want to compare different quantities over a period of time, or to display clearly the different amounts for a range of items.

Bar charts are also appropriate when there is more than one set of data to be compared. Each set of data will be represented by a different colour or shade of bar and description of these sets is contained within a legend. These different bars may be shown side by side or can be 'stacked' on top of each other if the total of these sets is also relevant.

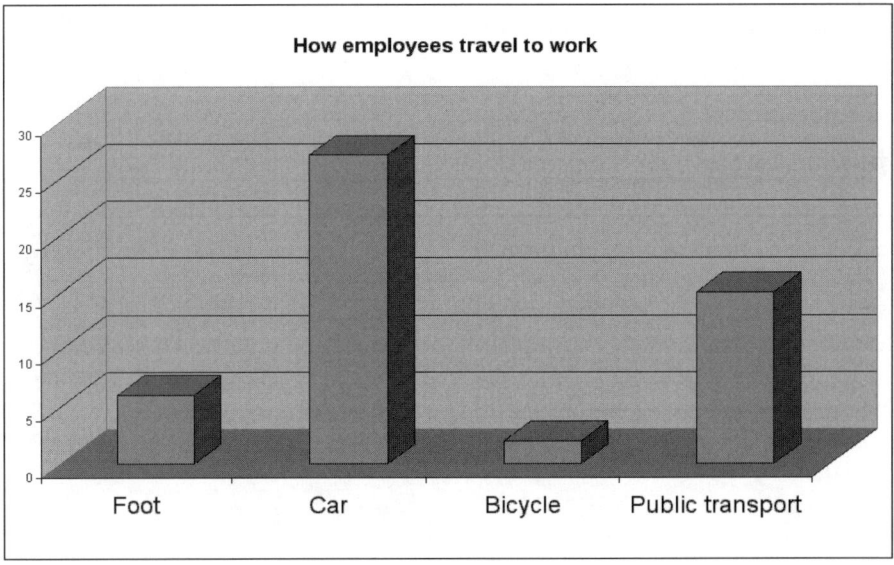

Figure 19 *A bar chart*

Line graph

When you want to show a *trend* in your data, it is often best to use a line graph. This type of graph shows a number of points joined together by a line. The use of the lines to join the points highlights the changes in the data values but the values between the points do not have a numerical significance. Line graphs, like bar charts, are frequently used with multiple data sets, showing several lines on the one chart.

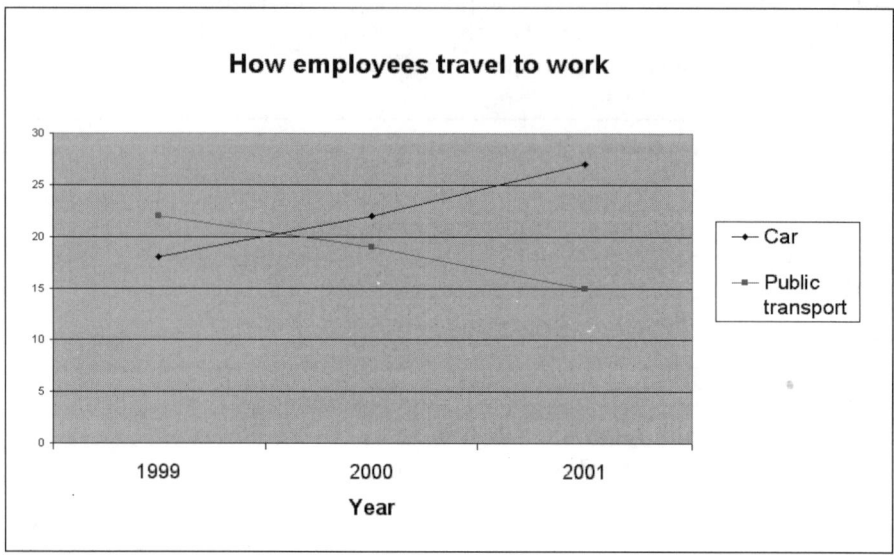

Figure 20   *A line graph*

Pie chart

Sometimes you may wish to display the relative frequencies of the data. This is done by calculating the frequencies as a share of the whole, most often by using percentages of the whole (each item's frequency divided by the total and multiplied by 100). Each frequency is represented as a portion of the whole 'pie', that is as a percentage of 360 degrees of a circle. This type of chart requires relatively complex calculations and is not easy to draw when using a pen and paper but, when using the spreadsheet package, all the hard work is done for you by the software. A pie chart can only represent one set of data.

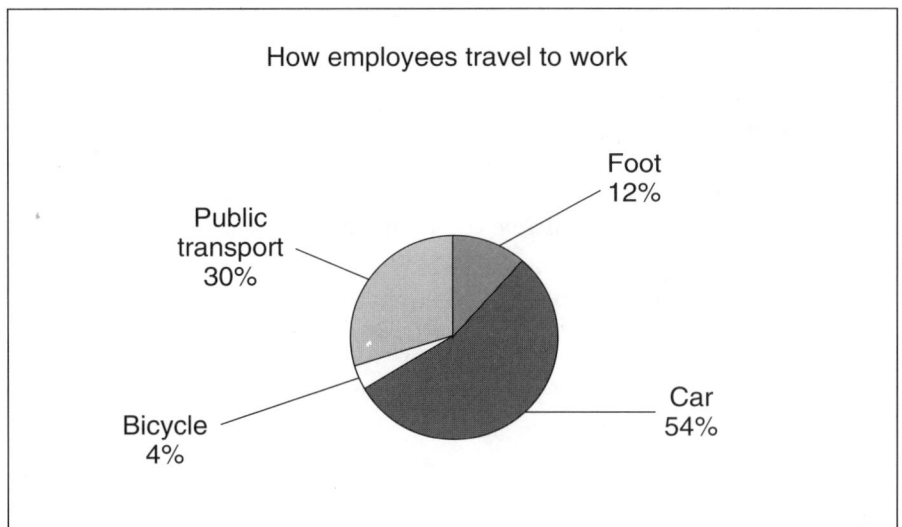

Figure 21   *A pie chart*

Chart annotation

Whatever type of chart is being produced, it is essential that it includes a title, data labels to identify the nature of the data and a legend where necessary. Both x and y axes need to have appropriate titles and the separation between bars, line or segments must be clearly defined. Whilst monochrome graphs can be effective in displaying the data pictorially through the use of patterns and shading, the use of colour will greatly enhance the final product.

CHECK IT YOURSELF

The spreadsheet checklist on p. 106 includes all the main graphical representation features you need to be able to use in your particular software. As you progress through the qualification, complete section 6 so that you can include this in your evidence folder as supplementary evidence.

Hard copy

For all the applications software that you use, you will need to know the output capabilities of the package. You will need to know all the parameters that need to be provided and how they operate with the particular equipment you are using. Modern laser printers are capable of carrying out many activities over and above simple printing (see p. 36).

You will need to make sure that you know how to control the output of your documents from the spreadsheet software. This will include double-sided printing, printing a specific page or range of pages, orientation of the page, and printing on different sizes and types of stationery. You may also be able to control the collation of multiple copies, including sorting and stapling.

Spreadsheet checklist

Section 1: layout features	
page size	
orientation	
margins	
headers and footers	
page numbering	
date and time stamp	
grid lines	
best fit	
text – font	
size	
emphasis	
colour	
borders	
shading	
Section 2: data formatting	
general	
decimal	
currency	
left	
right	
centre	
word wrap	
merge cells	
Section 3: calculations	
basic arithmetic (+, –, *, /)	
sum function	
average function	
median function	
mode function	
minimum function	

Spreadsheet checklist (continued)

maximum function	
count function	
Section 4: data manipulation	
copy	
move (cut and paste)	
insert	
delete	
sort	
Section 5: links	
links within a worksheet	
links to another worksheet	
links to other application	
export to other application	
Section 6: graphics	
pie chart	
line graph	
bar chart	
title	
data labels	
legends	

Case Study Activity

Information about the company Autoware has been included in the form of a case study on pp. 157–62. It describes the nature and structure of the organisation and will provide you with a context in which to carry out this task. It is therefore essential that you read this before you attempt this activity.

Gillian Bates, the Chief Executive of Autoware, has suggested to the Development Director, Marc Benoit, that it would be useful to have a 'ready-reckoner' to calculate the costs of development projects. It would be useful if this could be used on a project-by-project basis, but also provide summary information for development in a given financial year.

1. Each development project has a number of cost elements. There will be development staff costs, based on an average rate per day; sales staff costs, again on a rate per day; marketing staff costs for documentation production, based on a rate per day; management overheads – 1% of overall staff costs; travel, telephone and other communications costs.

2. You now need to design a spreadsheet solution to this problem. It should include:

   • layout of each sheet
   • formulae used
   • use of absolute cell references
   • data sheet links
   • detail and summary sheets
   • graphical representation of data.

Unit 311 Design and Use Databases

This unit contains three elements:

311.1 Design and create databases
311.2 Extract information by interrogating the database
311.3 Present the database information.

You need to demonstrate that you can interpret your customer's requirements to design database structures taking into account the facilities and constraints of the available resources. You will also need to demonstrate that you can adapt an existing database design where applicable. You will need to demonstrate that you can extract the required information from database files and carry out complex interrogations using a number of different methods. You will also need to show that you can correctly present extracted information in a variety of styles. This may include the use of facilities to create reports and also links to other applications.

To meet the requirements of this unit you should have a good understanding of the importance of thoroughly investigating the customer's requirements and of being able to work within imposed constraints. You will need to know a wide range of data interrogation methods including data relationships, complex queries and data sorting facilities within the database software. You will need to understand the factors affecting the choice of facilities and functions to meet the requirements. You will need to fully understand the factors affecting choice of presentation style when producing output from a database, including both screen- and paper-based output. You should also have a good understanding of the factors influencing your choice when linking the database information with other applications.

Database management system

Database management systems, DBMS, have been available on the desk top for some time and many people use them in a fairly basic way. However, most DBMS now have relational capability and can be used to provide far more powerful solutions.

In a relational DBMS the data is organised in such a way as to ensure the integrity of the data and to reduce unnecessary data redundancy. Data redundancy occurs where data is stored more than once. This can give rise to the potential for inconsistency between these different stores of the same data and therefore reduces the integrity of the data.

The structure of the database is organised into entities, also known as tables. An entity consists of a number of attributes, data items or fields, and may be related to another entity. Through the use of related entities, data redundancy is considerably reduced.

Let us look at an example of a simple order processing system. In a non-relational environment, sometimes referred to as a flat-file system, the data would look something like this:

Customer No	Customer Name	Customer Address	Order No	Order Date	Item Code	Description	Quantity
10076	Walls	High Rd	A1001	10/10/01	S234	A4 paper	20
98230	Patel	Long Lane	A1003	12/10/01	P981	envelopes	500
10076	Walls	High Rd	A1004	12/10/01	P981	envelopes	250
10076	Walls	High Rd	A1004	12/10/01	S267	staples	25
20467	Frost	Smith St	A1005	13/10/01	S876	paper clips	10

As you can see from the sample data, there is a lot of repetition, that is data redundancy.

In a relational design the same information may look something like this:

Customer No	Customer Name	Customer Address
10076	Walls	High Rd
20467	Frost	Smith St
98230	Patel	Long Lane

Customer

Customer No	Order No	Order Date
10076	A1001	10/10/01
98230	A1003	12/10/01
10076	A1004	12/10/01
20467	A1005	13/10/01

Order

Order No	Item Code	Description	Quantity
A1001	S234	A4 paper	20
A1003	P981	envelopes	500
A1004	P981	envelopes	250
A1004	S267	staples	25
A1005	S876	paper clips	10

Orderline

There is still some data redundancy but only that necessary to set up the relationships between the entities which enables the data to be linked.

Each entity needs to have a primary key field. The primary key will uniquely identify an individual record, for example each customer will have a unique Customer Number which would be used as the primary key for the entity CUSTOMER. For the entity ORDER, the Order Number will be unique for each new order and would be used as the primary key. In the entity ORDER LINE, neither the Order Number nor the Item Code on its own would be unique. If this was the case then an order could only have one item on it, which would not be very efficient, and an item could only ever be ordered once, which would not be good for business. The best way to ensure that the data is correctly related is by using **both** Order Number and Item Code as a composite primary key field.

The relationships between entities can be documented using an entity relationship diagram, an ERD.

Figure 22   *An entity relationship diagram*

Relationship definitions:

A Customer places one or many Orders but an Order is placed by one Customer only.

An Order contains one or many Order Lines but an Order Line is contained in one Order only.

It is now possible to access the related data from each of the entities with these relationships established.

Requirements specification

The design of the database is critical. A database is a complex solution and the specification will need to be quite detailed and include the data structure, data input, data processing and data output definitions.

The specification will need to identify the following:

- The purpose – what the database is going to be used for, eg order processing.
- The data sources – where is the data going to come from and is this internal or external to the organisation?
- The data items – every item of data to be used, eg customer name, customer address, etc.
- The characteristics of the data – data type, size and format.
- The methods of input – eg keyboard, mouse, etc.
- The layout of the input – what does the data look like at source and what will the input screens look like?
- The processes to be carried out on the data – any calculations, selections, manipulations.
- The recipients of the information – who is going to receive the information and when.
- The layout of the output – what do the screens and paper-based reports look like?
- The media for output – screen, paper, disk, etc.
- The hardware and software available – what platform is it to be developed and delivered on? What version of the software is available? Are colour prints required?

CHECK IT YOURSELF

You will need to find out all this information from your client. Sometimes it may be provided in a clear and precise way, but often it will not. You will need to record all of the requirements so that you can ensure that you meet the required specification. Design a pro-forma that will enable you to do this. It will need to record all of the above, and also enable you to identify any other information the client may consider to be important.

Design

Once you have identified the specification of requirements, you will then need to design the database. The first part of the system to be designed must be the structure of the data. This will determine how the other aspects can be achieved.

Your client will have identified the data items that are required. You now need to decide what entities are required, the attributes and fields that they contain and the characteristics of every data item. You should record your entity relationships using an ERD including written relationship definitions. You will need to identify the primary key field for each entity and ensure that that data item is also held in any related entity to enable the relationship to be established, known as the foreign key.

Data definition

The first thing you need to do is to identify precisely the structure of the data. You will need to make sure that the attributes you have identified will enable you to produce the information required. For example, consider the storage of names. How many attributes, i.e. fields, do you need?

one attribute:	NAME: Mr John Smith			
two attributes:	TITLE: Mr	NAME: John Smith		
three attributes:	TITLE: Mr	FIRST NAME: John	FAMILY NAME: Smith	
four attributes:	TITLE: Mr	FIRST NAME: John	FAMILY NAME: Smith	INITIAL: J

The more fields you have, the more storage space the data will occupy, but you will be able to use the data in a more flexible way. With only one field, without complex additional programming, you can only use the full name, and this may not always be suitable. You would not normally write *Dear Mr John Smith* at the start of a letter. With four fields you can address a letter as *Dear John* and the envelope with *Mr J Smith*. With the last two options, you can more easily sort the data alphabetically or select all the people with a FAMILY NAME of *Smith*.

Every data item will need to be given a fieldname. You will need to check the rules of your DBMS as to what this may consist of. It is also a good idea for you to adopt a convention on names. They need to be meaningful to make it easier to 'read' your definitions but may also include part of the table name. For example, Customer No in the CUSTOMER table may have the fieldname CCustomerNo whereas you call it OCustomerNo in the ORDER table.

Characteristics

You now need to identify the characteristics of each field:

- Data type   this indicates the type of data that can be held. You will need to know the types available within your DBMS, but you can expect to find text, numeric, date/time, currency and logical.

  The **text** data type should be used for a field that can contain any type of character.

  The **numeric** data type should only be used for *real* numbers, ie numbers that can be used in a calculation – a telephone number is *not* a real number, it is a code that happens to consist of digits but they do not have any numerical significance; telephone numbers should be set to a *text* data type.

  The **date** data type is extremely useful as it validates the date and so ensures that invalid dates cannot be entered; 29/02/02 will not be accepted but 29/02/04 will be.

- Field size   defines the maximum number of characters allowed in a text field. You will need to look at samples of data that will be held in each text field to decide on the field size; you also need to take into account likely future requirements so that the system does not need changing.

- Format   indicates how the data is to be displayed, eg the number of decimal places in a numeric field. For a date field, you need to decide whether to display the date as 28/04/02, or 28 Apr 02 or 28/04/2002, etc.

- Validation   is used where there are rules that you can include to reduce errors during data input, eg in the ORDER LINE entity, the quantity could never be less than 1.

As the process of designing and defining the data progresses, it becomes increasingly important to record this information. The entity and attribute data is collected and defined in a **data dictionary**. A simple, manually created data dictionary will usually provide an alphabetical listing of data items (attributes) and how they are combined to make up the table structures (entities) and will include their characteristics. Computerised data dictionaries can provide additional features for managing this data and may even be dynamic.

A simple data dictionary must include, for each entity:

- the name of each attribute
- the type of data
- the size of the data
- the format and/or any validation rules
- if it is a primary or foreign key.

The content of a data dictionary is known as **meta data** – data about data, it is the database designer's database. Relational database systems store data about the database in the same way as the actual database is held.

Table	Fieldname	Data type	Size	Format	Comments
Customer	CCustomerNo	Text	5	1 letter and 4 numbers	PRIMARY
	CCustomerName	Text	25	Initial capitals	Company name, so only one field
	CCustomer Address	Text	35		This might be divided into 2 or 3 separate fields so that data could also be used for mailing labels
Order	OCustomerNo	Text	5	1 letter and 4 numbers	Must be the same type and format as in the Customer table to establish the relationship
	OOrderNo	Text	4	1 letter and 3 numbers	PRIMARY
	OOrderDate	Date		Short date ie 15/09/2001	
Order Line	OLOrderNo	Text	4	1 letter and 3 numbers	Part PRIMARY Must be the same type and format as in the Order table to establish the relationship
	OLItemCode	Text	4	2 letters 2 numbers	Part PRIMARY
	OLDescription	Text	25	Initial capital	
	OLQuantity	Number		Integer	>=1

CHECK IT YOURSELF

The database checklist on p. 121 includes all the main data structure features you need to be able to use in your particular software. As you progress through the qualification, complete section 1 so that you can include this in your evidence folder as supplementary evidence.

Input layout

Now you have designed the data structure, you can decide what the input procedures look like. You need to draw up initial layouts for the screens to input the data. Remember, it is extremely important that your screens are 'user friendly'. This means that they are easy for the user to work with both in terms of the order in which the data is requested and in the colour scheme and general presentation of the screen. You will need to take into consideration your client's specific requirements and any standards and house styles that may exist.

You may decide to include techniques to improve the quality of the data input process, such as lists to choose from, combo-boxes, or boxes to be ticked. You can also use visual verification to improve the accuracy of the data. These should all be indicated in your layout designs.

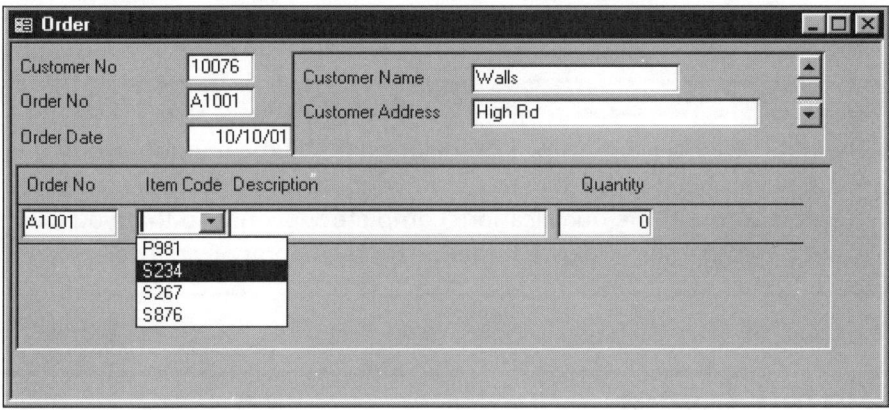

Figure 23 *Order input screen*

The Order input screen (Figure 23) has been designed so that when the Customer No is entered the Customer Name and Address are displayed for verification in a linked sub-form, and when the Order No is entered it is also automatically entered as the Order No in the linked OrderLine table so that all related entries will be correct.

To assist in entering the ordered items, a drop-down list of available codes is displayed in a combo-box for the user to pick from, sometimes referred to as a 'pick-list'.

The design view of this screen is shown in Figure 24. You can see the two sub-forms that are linked to the main form.

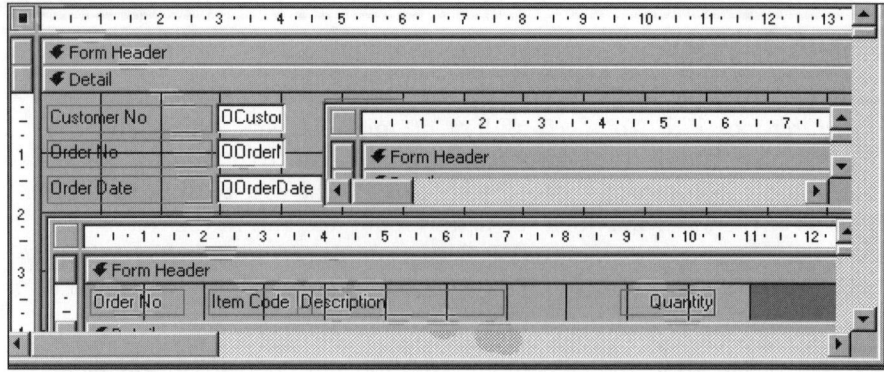

Figure 24 *Design view of the order input screen*

The controls that contain the data display the fieldnames but the associated labels can be any text you want. The combo-box can be seen with the drop-down arrow.

CHECK IT YOURSELF

The database checklist on p. 121 includes all the main input layout features you need to be able to use in your particular software. As you progress through the qualification, complete section 2 so that you can include this in your evidence folder as supplementary evidence.

Output layout

Again, you will need to produce designs of how any output screens may look, taking into consideration all the same issues as for the input screens. It is important to maintain an overall 'look and feel' to the database and this can be achieved by consistency in your screen layouts. You will also need to design any paper-based outputs. They will need to conform to organisational house styles and you will need to ensure that they contain all the required information, and in a 'user friendly' format.

You will need to consider whether these outputs are for *internal* or *external* users, as the format and presentation issues are different.

Internal outputs are intended for internal systems owners and systems users. They are rarely used outside of the organisation and are produced to support the day-to-day business operations, to assist management monitoring the business and in decision making. They may be:

- detailed reports – with little or no selection or restrictions to the data
- summary reports – categorises information for managers who do not need to have to look at all the detail (totals and statistics are often included)

- exception reports – only includes information about exceptional events, eg outstanding account balances greater than a specified value.

External outputs are intended to leave the organisation and are designed to be used by customers, suppliers and the general public. They are usually produced to conclude or report on a business transaction.

The design of the output should ensure that they are simple to read and interpret.

- Every output should have a title – for reference purposes.
- Every output should be date and time stamped – shows currency.
- Reports and screens should include sections and headings to segment information – greater clarity.
- Form-based output, all fields should be clearly labelled.
- In tabular-based output, columns should be clearly labelled on every page.
- Only required information should be included.
- Information should not require to be edited further after output.
- A balanced output will improve readability.
- Users need to be able to navigate around the information easily and quickly.

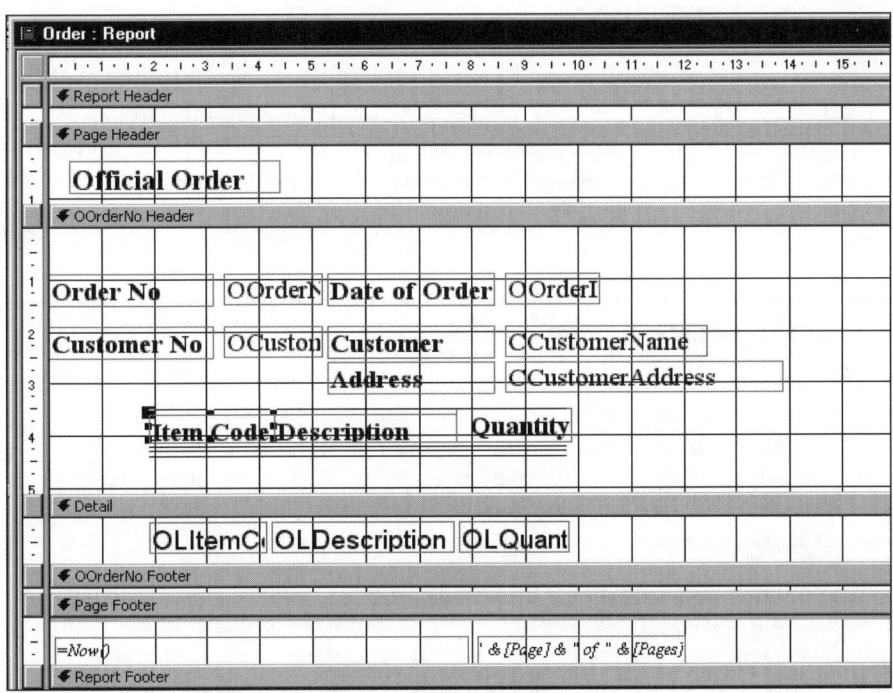

Figure 25 *Sample report layout*

The DBMS will have a Report Generator facility that will help you create paper-based output. This will let you define the fields to be printed and the order in which they are to be displayed. There will be facilities to change the order in which the records are printed and to group sets of records into different sections within the report. It will also let you specify headers or footers to fit the structure of your report.

Official Order			
Order No	A1001	Date of Order	10/10/01
Customer No	10076	Customer	Walls
		Address	High Rd
Item Code	Description	Quantity	
S234	A4 paper	20	

Figure 26   *Sample report output*

CHECK IT YOURSELF

The database checklist on p. 121 includes all the main output layout features you need to be able to use in your particular software. As you progress through the qualification, complete section 3 so that you can include this in your evidence folder as supplementary evidence.

Interrogation methods

It is likely that the main reason that you will have decided to use a DBMS to provide a solution to your client's problem is so that large volumes of related data can be stored, interrogated and manipulated to provide the required information. You will need to agree with your client the data manipulation and interrogation required, recording it as part of the specification of the database.

The language SQL (structured query language) was developed specifically to provide an industry-standard interrogation tool that could be used on any relational database. This language, with minor variations for different suppliers, is now in general use. However, you do not need to know this language to work with many database packages. The DBMS will usually support SQL and will have a query-by-example (QBE) screen to help you construct the code, often without you even needing to be aware of it!

This screen will let you identify the tables that you wish to use and will recognise any relationships you have already established. You should also be able to set up relationships between tables that are defined solely for the purposes of this specific query. You can then select the required fields to be included and identify your selection criteria. It is also possible to define sort criteria to organise the data into the required order.

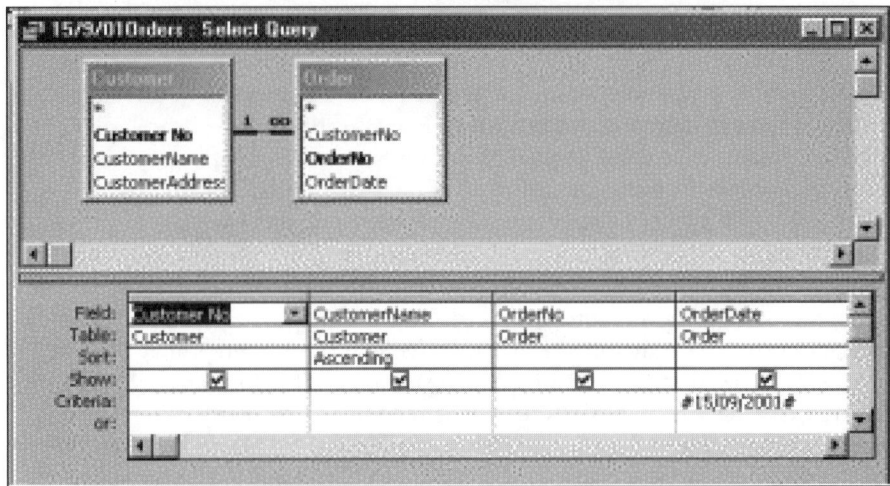

Figure 27 *Select query*

The query shown in Figure 27 uses the Customer and Order tables and uses the one-to-many relationship between them. The Customer No and Customer Name have been taken from the Customer table together with the Order No and Order Date from the Order table. The Sort criteria has been set to Ascending on the Customer Name and the Selection criteria to Order Date = 15/9/2001.

This query will display, in the form of an answer table, one record (row) for each order placed on the 15/9/2001 giving the Customer No and the Customer Name from the Customer table and the Date and Order No from the Order table. The default table display is not usually very 'user friendly'; you can display the results of these queries either on the screen by creating a Form, or on paper by creating a Report.

Links

There are many occasions when the data in a database needs to be made available for use in another application. For example, a spreadsheet may contain comparative data, possibly from an external source, and spreadsheet software is more suitable for this type of data manipulation. You therefore need to *export* a subset of your database to carry out this activity. Database data can be exported in a *comma delimited* format. The resulting file will contain the data items from each record of the selected data table, separated by commas. Each new record will start on a new line, that is there will be a carriage return code included in the file. Where there is an empty field, one comma will be immediately followed by another. This format may also be referred to as **csv** format. This format is recognised by many different applications packages as it is the industry standard for exporting data. There may also be the facility to export the data table directly to the spreadsheet format that you use.

The comma delimited, or csv, file can also be *imported* into a word processing document. Most word processing packages will insert this data into a table, with one column for each field and one row for each record. A data table can also be exported in a format that can be used in a word processing package for mail merge (see p. 84). If you are working within a suite of software, the specific merge format may be explicitly available, but the csv format will usually also be understood by the mail merge facility of the word processor.

Database checklist

Section 1: data structures	
tables	
relationships	
primary key	
foreign key	
field	
fieldname	
data type	
field size	
data format	
data validation	
Section 2: input design	
screen layout	
form	
colour	
design view	
combo-boxes	
tick boxes	
sub-form	
Section 3: output design	
screen layout	
report generator	
groups	
headers and footers	
Section 4: interrogation methods	
QBE	
single selection criterion	
multiple selection criteria	
AND/OR	
sort	
Section 5: links	
exported data	
mail merge	

Case Study Activity

Information about the company Autoware has been included in the form of a case study on pp. 157–62. It describes the nature and structure of the organisation and will provide you with a context in which to carry out this task. It is therefore essential that you read this before you attempt this activity.

Autoware would like to revise its database system for tracking customers' licences. A customer will have purchased a licence for a specified number of users which it can increase with an amendment to the licence agreement. The customer also has a maintenance agreement, which is renewed annually and is also based on the number of users.

1. You have been asked to carry out an initial design of this database. You will need to decide what tables are needed, the fields within each of these tables and to identify primary and foreign keys. To describe your design you will need to produce an entity relationship diagram and table definitions identifying all the fields' characteristics.

2. You then need to design input screen layouts for the following:

   - to input new licence agreements
   - to input maintenance contract renewals
   - to display the results of a query on a specific customer and its licence and maintenance contract status.

Unit 312 Design and Produce Documents Using Graphics

This unit contains three elements:

312.1 Design the layout and presentation of graphical documents
312.2 Create the required graphical documents
312.3 Output graphical document to the required destination.

You need to demonstrate that you can interpret your customer's requirements to design graphical document layouts taking into account the facilities and constraints of the available resources, and particularly the use of appropriate input devices. You will also need to demonstrate that you can adapt existing designs where applicable. You will need to demonstrate that you are competent in producing a variety of complex graphical documents, using facilities to format, manipulate and establish dynamic links where applicable for the required documents. You will also need to show that you can correctly identify appropriate output devices and output parameters to produce the required graphical documents.

To meet the requirements of this unit you should have a good understanding of the importance of thoroughly investigating the customer's requirements and of being able to work within imposed constraints, particularly regarding the range of input devices available. You will need to know a wide range of facilities within the graphics software and the factors affecting the choice of facilities and functions to meet the requirements for the documents. You should have a good understanding of the factors affecting your choice of output device and the importance of ensuring confidentiality of the information.

Introduction

There are a number of types of graphical documents that you need to know about, although you may be working primarily with only one type.

There are the documents produced to meet the technical drawing requirements for engineering disciplines such as mechanical engineering, and particularly within the motor industry, architecture, the various areas of construction and electronic engineering and also in the field of printed circuit board design and computer manufacture. These needs are met through the use of CAD (computer-aided design) packages. This type of drawing software is designed to produce diagrams that show the exact physical dimensions and the precise details such that they can be used to manufacture the object.

3D graphics is primarily used to view a design idea or concept from all angles, as if it actually existed. Engineers, architects and product designers use this type of application to model their designs. An architect may create this type of image so that a client can 'walk through' the building, even though it has not yet been built.

Another, very different, graphical document requirement arises in the areas of graphic design and art. Here the need is for software that will facilitate the creation of graphical images for inclusion in magazines, videos, advertisements, websites etc., and even art galleries.

Vector (object-oriented) graphics

The diagrams produced in a CAD package will be created using vector graphics. This is based on a precise mathematical description of the picture, in which each object, a line, a circle, etc., is represented by a mathematical equation of the object itself. This gives this type of software incredible potential and flexibility. When the user zooms in on a part of the drawing, the image to be displayed is recalculated, using the equation, to accurately increase the size of that part of the diagram. This means that, theoretically, this type of software has an unlimited zoom; you can zoom in to infinity, there is no limit to the enlargement of an object, and this is exactly what is required in the technical drawing applications.

As the objects within a vector graphics application consist of mathematical equations that describe the object, this provides the software with all the necessary information to carry out calculations about the object. So, for example, it is possible to calculate the area or volume of the object, or the mass of that object when manufactured in a specified material.

Whilst these types of images do not require high volumes of data storage, the mathematical processing required to generate and re-generate the images is quite considerable and, to operate effectively, requires powerful processing capabilities.

Bitmap graphics

By contrast, bitmap images are created in pixels and consist of blocks of colour. Most artwork packages create this type of graphical document. When you render a vector graphics image, to make it appear solid, bitmap or raster graphics are used to provide the blocks of colour.

Bitmap images will tend to be much larger and have a limited zoom.

Design specification

The design for a graphical document needs to be recorded so that you have a clear definition against which to assess how closely you have met the client's requirements.

The specification will need to identify the following:

- The purpose – what the graphical document will be used for, eg company logo, wheel design, etc.
- The layout of the document – there may be standards defining the format of the document, eg the title block in a technical document.
- The graphics protocol – eg 1st angle orthographic, isometric, 3D, wire-frame, rendered, etc.
- Research information – indicating, for example, target group preferences, market information, etc.
- The contents of the document – this will vary enormously depending on the type of document.
- The recipients of the information – who is going to receive the information and when?
- The media for output – paper, transparencies, film, disk, etc.
- The hardware and software available – what platform is it to be developed and delivered on? What version of the software is available? Are colour prints required?

CHECK IT YOURSELF

You will need to find out all this information from your client. Sometimes it may be provided in a clear and precise way, but often it will not. You will need to record all of the requirements so that you can ensure that you meet the required specification. Design a pro-forma that will enable you to do this. It will need to record all of the above, and also enable you to identify any other information the client may consider to be important.

Design

Once you have agreed the specification with your client, you need to design the layout of the graphical document. For many technical requirements, this will be the implementation of the specification, however for the graphic design type brief you will need to go through a design process. A method, known as storyboarding, is frequently used for this. A storyboard is a sequence of designs, or sketches, that show the ideas for layouts, the positioning of the content and the colours and techniques to be used.

Page 1 – Layout and content	Format etc	
Title – Using The Printer	*Title font:*	16 pt, Arial black, left aligned, initial capitals
diagram of printer with main parts numbered	*Graphics:*	printer.jpg, centred, black border
names of parts related to numbers on diagram	*Text font:*	11 pt, Arial black, two columns, left aligned, numbered list

Page 2 – Layout and content	Format etc	
Title – Loading Paper	*Title font:*	14 pt, Arial black, left aligned, initial capitals
close-up diagram of paper trays showing position of paper for loading	*Graphics:*	paper.jpg, centred, black border
step-by-step description of paper loading process	*Text font:*	11 pt, Arial black, numbered list, left aligned

Figure 28 *An example of a storyboard*

There will be many factors to be included in this storyboard. There will be issues regarding the actual images; your client will need to be presented with a range of alternatives using various techniques such as drawings, clip-art, photographs and existing artwork. There will need to be a consideration of colour schemes and textures, and the general style of the document.

You will need to present your storyboard to your client, possibly at a meeting, so that you can formally agree the design of the graphical document. It is extremely important that this takes place *before* you start to do the development. Your client may have very strong views about what is required, even though he or she may have initially given you a very open brief, and you could waste a lot of time doing work that is not acceptable.

In some organisations, there may be a formal acceptance document to confirm the agreement by the client. This can be very important as the client may change his or her mind during the development stages and you need any alterations to be acknowledged as amendments to the original agreed design as this might affect your completion date.

Are there formal agreement procedures in your organisation? Find out what these are and, if these are in a written document, place a copy in your evidence folder as supplementary evidence. If they are not written out, write out your own copy to place in your evidence folder, getting confirmation from your line manager that it is correct.

Page layout

One of the first considerations when designing a document will be regarding the layout of the whole page. You will need to take into account the requirements of your client but also the constraints and limitations that may be imposed by the available software and output facilities.

- Page size

  If you are using a laser printer or ink jet printer it will usually be A4 (210 × 297 mm or 8.27 × 11.69 in) although you may also use Legal (8.5 × 14 in) or Letter (8.5 × 11 in). Some printers may also be able to handle A3 or even A5 paper. Particularly in a CAD environment your output could be to a pen plotter which would usually handle paper up to A0 (840 × 1188 mm).

- Orientation

  You will need to decide the orientation of the pages, portrait or landscape. Sometimes, for example when printing part of a drawing, you may need to adjust the orientation for best fit on the page.

- Margins

  The usable area on the page in which you can place the main part of your document is controlled by setting the size of the four margins – top, bottom, left and right. This will also be constrained by the output device as this usually will not print to the edge of the page.

The graphical document checklist on p. 131 includes all the main layout features you need to be able to use in your particular software. As you progress through the qualification, complete section 1 so that you can include this in your evidence folder as supplementary evidence.

Attributes

- Colour

  In vector graphic applications, colour will usually be specified by layer or object whereas in bitmap applications the colour of each pixel is defined.

- Line type

  There will be a range of solid and broken line types available to choose from.

- Line thickness

  You will be able to define the thickness of any given line. In some packages this choice can be as great as from 0 to infinity. However, the processing power required to draw a line of infinite thickness would not be available and, therefore, great care must be taken when using this feature.

CHECK IT YOURSELF

The graphical document checklist on p. 131 includes all the main attributes you need to be able to define in your particular software. As you progress through the qualification, complete section 2 so that you can include this in your evidence folder as supplementary evidence.

Manipulation of images

An image, or part of an image, can be manipulated in a number of different ways.

- Size

  The size can be increased or decreased both by dragging and by a defined amount. This change can be made to maintain the aspect ratio or to allow distortion.

- Orientation

  An image can be rotated or mirrored around a specified point. If this is copied as an array, the image can be copied and rotated about a central point, for example when drawing teeth on a gear wheel only one tooth needs to be drawn (see Figure 29).

- Cropping

  You can edit an image using the technique known as cropping. This is where you can trim a picture on both the vertical and horizontal edges, to extract the required part. You can usually un-crop a picture if necessary.

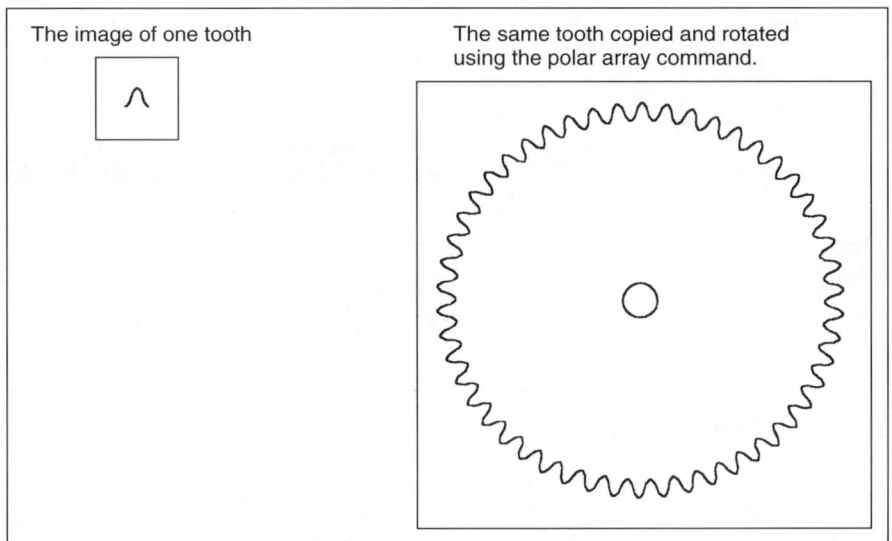

Figure 29 *Image orientation*

CHECK IT YOURSELF

The graphical document checklist on p. 131 includes all the main image manipulation you need to be able to carry out in your particular software. As you progress through the qualification, complete section 3 so that you can include this in your evidence folder as supplementary evidence.

Text

- Font
  The shape and style of the text can be varied enormously. Most printers will support a considerable number of different fonts. Some are very plain and clear and therefore more appropriate for business applications, while others are much more fancy and elaborate and are very effective for less formal communications or possibly for posters and leaflets.

- Size
  Not only can you use different fonts, but you can also control the size. With printers capable of producing very high-quality print, it is not only possible to print very small, fine characters quite clearly but also to print very large letters. Most fonts are measured in points – the bigger the number, the larger the character.

- Orientation

  In many graphics packages you will be able to rotate or flip the text just like any other object.

CHECK IT YOURSELF

The graphical document checklist on p. 131 includes all the main text facilities you need to be able to use in your particular software. As you progress through the qualification, complete section 4 so that you can include this in your evidence folder as supplementary evidence.

Automation facilities

A frequently used object, or group of objects, can be defined and named. Whenever this image is required, the user-defined named object can be used. In some applications this may be referred to as a macro.

Where a series of graphical documents are being produced, for example when producing a set of drawings for a user manual, or where there are organisation standards, such as for technical drawings with borders and title block to a specified layout, a template for the document can be set up to speed up the process and ensure consistency.

CHECK IT YOURSELF

The graphical documents checklist on page 131 includes all the main automation facilities you need to be able to use in your particular software. As you progress through the qualification, complete section 5 so that you can include this in your evidence folder as supplementary evidence.

Hard copy

For all the applications software that you use, you will need to know the output capabilities of the package. You will need to know all the parameters that need to be provided and how they operate with the particular equipment you are using. Modern laser printers are capable of carrying out many activities over and above simple printing (see p. 36). You may also be using a pen plotter and will need to know how to configure your software so that it produces the correct type of output, using the right colours.

You will need to make sure that you know how to control the output of your documents from the graphics software. This will include double-sided printing, printing a specific page or range of pages, orientation of the page, and printing on different sizes and types of stationery. You may also be able to control the collation of multiple copies, including sorting and stapling.

Graphical document checklist

Section 1: page layout features	
page size	
orientation	
margins	
Section 2: attributes	
colour	
line type	
line thickness	
Section 3: manipulation of images	
size	
orientation	
copy	
delete	
insert	
Section 4: text	
font	
size	
orientation	
Section 5: automated facilities	
templates	
macros	

Case Study Activity

Information about the company Autoware has been included in the form of a case study on pp. 157–62. It describes the nature and structure of the organisation and will provide you with a context in which to carry out this task. It is therefore essential that you read this before you attempt this activity.

Autoware has a very active website. Gillian Bates, the Chief Executive, believes that the web plays a very important role in putting across the image of the company. The web master is very proud of the quality of the site and places considerable emphasis upon the importance of design.

Some new pages are being created which will focus on the software systems that are designed specifically for the motorcycle industry. It has been agreed that, whilst it is essential to maintain an overall company style across all parts of the site, these pages need also to appeal to the targeted part of the market.

1. There are many sites that are directed to the motorcycle enthusiast. Carry out some research into the style and structure of some of these sites and to identify some key components that may be appropriate for Autoware to include.

2. You now need to identify, with particular consideration to the graphics, ideas for the motorcycle section of the software house website. You should use storyboarding techniques to present your ideas. You need to include a number of different ideas and each must include:

    *   types of graphics
    *   size of graphics
    *   positioning of graphics
    *   colours
    *   text styles.

Unit 326 Design and Produce Presentations Using Information Technology

This unit contains three elements:

326.1 Design the layout of the presentation
326.2 Create the required presentation
326.3 Demonstrate the presentation.

You need to demonstrate that you can interpret your customer's requirements to design presentation layouts taking into account the facilities and constraints of the available resources. You will need to demonstrate that you are competent in producing a variety of complex presentations, using facilities to format, manipulate, structure and establish dynamic links where applicable for the required presentations and will need to show that you can correctly identify appropriate input devices. You will also need to demonstrate that you can identify opportunities to improve the design and production of presentations, presenting your recommendations to the relevant person. You will need to instruct your customer on how to install and deliver the presentation show, and write simple but complete instruction notes.

To meet the requirements of this unit, you should have a good understanding of the importance of thoroughly investigating the customer's requirements and of being able to work within imposed constraints. You will need to know a wide range of facilities within the presentation software and the factors affecting the choice of facilities and functions to meet the requirements for the presentations. You will need to fully appreciate the facilities available for animation, rehearsed timings, sound and slide transition to enhance the effectiveness of a presentation show. You will need to understand the range and use of dynamic links to other applications and hyperlinks. You will also need to understand how to provide clear and simple installation instructions, both orally and in writing.

Introduction

Presentation software has significantly changed the way that many people design and deliver formal presentations. Presentations would usually be carried out with the use of an overhead projector and transparencies that were often produced by photocopying from paper onto an acetate sheet. With the use of a computer connected to a projector, it is now possible to produce high quality materials that use a wide range of interactive presentation techniques to pace the information displayed to match the speed of the speaker. It is also possible to run the presentation without a presenter using pre-set, automatic timings.

Specification

The design of the presentation is critical. There are many factors to be considered over and above the usual range that need to be taken into account when handling any information. A presentation will usually consist of a number of related slides or pages of information. These slides will need to put forward a coherent and concise message, and to do this will need to have clarity of information and a consistency of style.

The specification will need to identify the following:

- The topic – the title of the presentation will usually identify the focus.
- The purpose – eg this may be an information-giving presentation or a sales demonstration.
- The audience – who is going to receive this? Are they from within the organisation or external? Are they senior members of the organisation? Do they have previous knowledge about the topic?
- The time it should last – this may affect how many slides are used and any automatic timings.
- The method of presentation – will it be interactive using a computer projector or output onto acetates for use with an overhead projector?
- The image to be projected – what the tone to be set is and whether humour is appropriate. Should there be an emphasis on facts and figures, or is this about raising awareness and encouraging discussion?
- The content – this may include the exact text, the images to be used, colour schemes required, etc., or it may offer you varying levels of design flexibility.
- The media – is the finished product to be provided on disk, floppy or possibly CD? Will acetates be required?
- The hardware and software available – what platform is it to be developed and delivered on? What version of the software is available? Are colour prints required?
- The documentation – will presentation notes be required? Is the audience to receive handouts?

You will need to find out all this information from your client. Sometimes it may be provided in a clear and precise way, but often it will not. You will need to record all of the requirements so that you can ensure that you meet the required specification. Design a pro-forma that will enable you to do this. It will need to record all of the above, and also enable you to identify any other information the client may consider to be important.

Layout

Once you have agreed the specification with your client, you need to design the layout of the presentation. A method, known as storyboarding, is frequently used for this. A storyboard is a sequence of screen designs, or sketches, that show the layout of each screen, the positioning of the content, the colours and images used and how each screen progresses to the next. It will therefore identify the links and transition features used, including timings and build features.

You will need to present your storyboard to your client, possibly at a meeting, so that you can formally agree the design of the presentation. It is extremely important that this takes place *before* you start to do the development. Your client may have very strong views about what is required, even though he or she may have initially given you a very open brief, and you could waste a lot of time doing work that is not acceptable.

Slide 1 – Layout and content	Format and actions
NVQ 3 – Using IT About the NVQ What is it? • An NVQ (National Vocational Qualification) is a set of work-based standards. • An NVQ consists of a number of units. • A unit consists of a number of elements	*Heading font:* Comic Sans MS – 32 pt black, centred *Body text font:* Arial – 26 pt black, left *Bullet text font:* Arial – 24 pt black, left *Bullet style:* small black, left *Background colour:* mid blue *Background wallpaper:* none *Slide build:* fly from left *Graphics:* none *Header:* none *Footer:* production date and page number

Slide 2	Format and actions
What is a portfolio?	*Transition*: dissolve
The evidence collection	*Heading Font*: Comic Sans MS – 32 pt black, centred
What will it contain?	
• Printouts, etc., the end products	*Body text font*: Arial – 26 pt black, left
• Witness statements	*Bullet text font*: Arial – 24 pt black, left
• Reports and other documents	*Bullet style*: small black
• It will be organised and indexed	*Background colour*: mid blue
	Background wallpaper: none
	Graphics: portfolio.gif
	Header: none
	Footer: production date and page number
	Slide build: fly from left

(Graphic placed in the Slide 2 column)

In some organisations, there may be a formal acceptance document to confirm the agreement by the client. This can be very important as the client may change his or her mind during the development stages and you need any alterations to be acknowledged as amendments to the original agreed design as this might affect your completion date.

CHECK IT YOURSELF

Are there formal agreement procedures in your organisation? Find out what these are and, if these are in a written document, place a copy in your evidence folder as supplementary evidence. If they are not written out, write out your own copy to place in your evidence folder, getting confirmation from your line manager that it is correct.

A presentation slide can contain many of the layout features of any document. You can include headers and footers and page numbers, use a range of fonts and adjust the size of the text used. In a presentation, the other important layout consideration is the colour scheme and background to be used. By setting up a master page, you can ensure that this layout is applied to all the slides in the presentation.

Graphical images

An important part of many presentations is the use of graphical images. These images may come from many sources and be in many different formats. The wide selection of 'clip-art' available can often provide appropriate and sometimes amusing graphics to liven up a presentation. It is also not uncommon to need to include the company logo, which is usually available as a graphic file. Many presentation packages will have available additional tools to assist in the creation of bar charts and organisation charts. You will need to familiarise yourself with all these features and how to manipulate these images.

Presentation show

One of the most powerful aspects of presentation software is the ability to make it interactive. This is achieved using a range of techniques.

Animation

A presentation can be made to have a greater impact with the use of animation. Within the context of presentations, this means 'building' each slide one element at a time, as it is required. When working with an acetate and an overhead projector, this could only be achieved by placing a piece of paper on the slide and moving it down to reveal each point as it was required, which is not really very professional in appearance.

For each slide, the elements to be added are specified, and the order in which they are to appear is defined. The way in which they are added is then specified and may include effects such as *dissolve, zoom, flash, appear* and *fly*. Many of these effects will have further qualifying definitions such as whether they happen *fast, medium* or *slow*, or to specify the direction from which they will appear. When the element is displayed, it can be accompanied by an appropriate sound. There will usually be a number of predefined sounds available with the package but you will also be able to add your own.

Action buttons can be placed onto the presentation and have action settings assigned that will run when the button is 'clicked'. This may be to go to another slide within the presentation or to link to another application.

Slide transitions

As part of the definition of a presentation, you can identify different effects to be used to move from one slide to another. There will be a range of these transitions to choose from within your package and you should be able to specify the speed at which they take place. You can also assign a sound effect to accompany the change to a new slide.

Timings

You can set up the slide show, for both the animation and slide transition effects, to run whenever the left mouse button is clicked. However, you can also set it up so that it runs on pre-set timings. You can allocate a time delay as each element is added, and you can also define the time delay before the transition to the next slide. This means that you can set the show to run automatically. However, it is extremely important to get these timings right and there will be a tool available so that you can rehearse the timings and adjust the presentation to accommodate any required alterations.

Links

Some of the information to be made available to the audience may be contained in another application. This may be a document that exists as a word processing file, a set of data that is held in a spreadsheet file or perhaps a chart in a spreadsheet file. There will be occasions when you only need to present a 'snap-shot' view of this information and then you can use the 'clip-board', using the copy and paste features, in the usual way. However, there may also be situations when the presentation will be used on a number of occasions, for example it could be used each month at the sales meeting to present the current sales figures. In this sort of application, the data will need to be linked dynamically. This means that whenever the data changes it will be automatically updated in your presentation. Dynamic links can also be set up to go to the required application and display the actual document or file.

Hyperlinks

A hyperlink is an object which, when 'clicked', jumps the control to another object. You can add a hyperlink to your presentation and then use it to go to a variety of locations – for example a specific slide within your presentation, a different presentation altogether, a word processing or spreadsheet document, an Internet, intranet, or e-mail address. You can create a hyperlink from any object – including text, shapes, tables, graphs, and pictures.

CHECK IT YOURSELF

The presentation software checklist on p. 141 includes all the main automation and linking features you need to be able to use in your particular software. As you progress through the qualification, complete section 3 so that you can include this in your evidence folder as supplementary evidence.

Presentation documentation

The text, images and data that are displayed on the slides will not include every word that the presenter needs to use. They are very much the prompts and key words that need to be visually available to the receiving group. The presenter will also need a set of presentation notes to accompany them. The software you use will have a facility to attach notes to each slide which can be printed out for use by the presenter (see Figure 30).

The audience will often appreciate a paper-based record of the presentation. There will usually be a facility to print the slides as a handout. This handout can be printed in colour, greyscale or black and white. You will also be able to choose how many slides appear on a page, usually 2, 4 or 6.

NVQ 3 – Using IT

About the NVQ

What is it?

• An NVQ (National Vocational Qualification) is a set of work-based standards.

• An NVQ consists of a number of units.

• A unit consists of a number of elements.

About the NVQ
What is it?
An NVQ (National Vocational Qualification) is a specification that has been set by a national training organisation to define the work-based standards. The organisation for IT is the Information Technology National Training Organisation (ITNTO).

An NVQ consists of a number of units. A unit is a complete section of knowledge and skills.

Each unit is broken down into a number of elements which are described by a set of performance criteria. These spell out the things you have to do and the skills and knowledge you need to demonstrate.

You are assessed against these standards and are required to demonstrate your competence for all the performance criteria and across a specified range (the scope and the variety) of activities.

1

Figure 30   *Notes accompanying a slide*

CHECK IT YOURSELF

The presentation software checklist on p. 141 includes all the main presentation documentation facilities you need to be able to use in your particular software. As you progress through the qualification, complete section 4 so that you can include this in your evidence folder as supplementary evidence.

Presentation software checklist

Section 1: layout features	
page size	
orientation	
margins	
headers and footers	
page numbering	
paragraph justification	
master page	
background colour	
text – font	
size	
emphasis	
colour	
justification	
bulleted lists	
tables	
Section 2: graphical images	
'clip-art'	
graphic files	
size	
bar charts	
organisation charts	
Section 3: presentation show	
animation	
slide transition	
timings	
links	
hyperlinks	
Section 4: presentation documentation	
slides	
handouts	
presenter's notes	

Information about the company Autoware has been included in the form of a case study on pp. 157–62. It describes the nature and structure of the organisation and will provide you with a context in which to carry out this task. It is therefore essential that you read this before you attempt this activity.

Autoware Chief Executive, Gillian Bates, has noticed that whilst it is common practice for organisations to have clearly defined house styles for all their main methods of communication, the presentation is rarely included. At Autoware the use of presentation software is mandatory for this type of activity, but each presenter adopts his or her own style. The Chief Executive has decided that it is time for presentations to be brought into company standards.

1. A wide variety of approaches is available for presentations, with the software offering a range of suggested styles. Carry out research as to the different styles available and explore their relevance to the organisation.

2. Create a style guide for Autoware presentations. It will need to include the following:

   - types of graphics
   - colour schemes
   - use of logos, etc.
   - fonts, sizes, etc.
   - build techniques
   - transition methods
   - presenter's notes
   - handouts.

Unit 327 Control the Use of Electronic Communication

This unit contains four elements:

327.1 Select and configure electronic communications for use
327.2 Transmit data using electronic communications
327.3 Receive data using electronic communications
327.4 Retrieve electronically stored information effectively.

You need to demonstrate that you can select and configure electronic communication resources. You will need to use computer-generated facsimile facilities, electronic mail and electronic information services to meet the customer's requirements.

To meet the requirements of this unit you should have a good understanding of the types of electronic communication resources available and the factors that affect the configuration of these resources. You will need to be aware of the legislation relating to the transmission and retrieval of information and the issues of confidentiality that arise through the use of this technology.

The resources for electronic communications

Hardware

Most modern computer equipment will have the capability for electronic communications. If the electronic communications link involves the use of a standard telephone line, then you will need to have a modem. The word modem is constructed from the words **mod**ulator and **dem**odulator. A modem turns computer data into a type and level of signal that is suitable for transmission on the telephone line. A similar modem is required at the receiving end, carrying out the reverse process, as shown in Figure 31.

Most computers now include a built-in modem as part of the standard configuration. To connect to a local network you will also need to have a network card installed in the computer.

Software

Each different type of electronic communication will require its own communications software. This software will need to be installed and

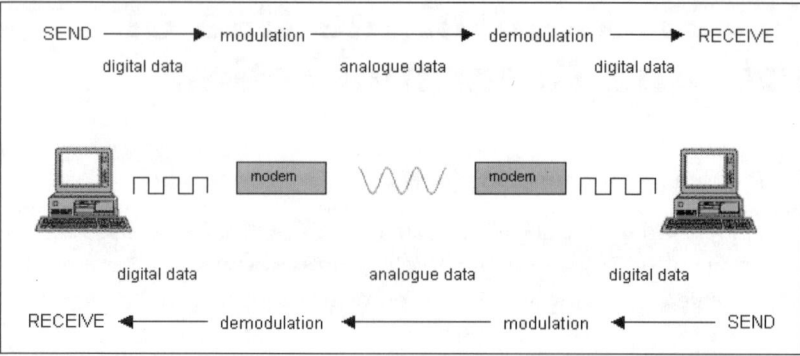

Figure 31 *How a modem works*

configured to meet the specific needs. E-mail software may include computer-based fax facilities, and a local area network will need network software such as NT or Novel netware. To access the Internet you will need an Internet browser.

Communication links

Most stand-alone computer connections will be carried out using a standard telephone line and a modem. However, this provides a relatively slow connection which is subject to all the vagaries of the telephone system, particularly regarding the quality of the line. An ISDN (Integrated Services Digital Network) connection is now commonly used by small businesses and is also available in the home. This provides faster transmission speeds of a higher quality and can handle audio and video data.

Where high speed transmission is required, cable and satellite systems are usually used to provide the connection, but new developments such as ASDL (Asymmetric Digital Subscriber Line) and VDSL (Very fast high data rate Digital Subscriber Line) have the potential to compete with these services, providing megabit speeds to home users.

Facsimile facilities

Facsimile, usually referred to as fax, is the transmission of exact copies of documents across the telephone network and has become one of the standard ways of making key documents available almost anywhere in the world. Any document, whether it is handwritten, contains pictures, diagrams, graphs, charts or typed text, can be transmitted at great speed for relatively low costs. Fax facilities are now also becoming a standard feature of computer-based electronic communication systems.

There are many benefits to most organisations in using fax, including the following:

- The speed of transmission is almost instant and does not depend on a third party for delivery.
- It is widely available – most organisations have fax receiving facilities.
- The cost of transmission, particularly when speed and reliability are taken into account, is relatively low.
- International standards exist to ensure worldwide capability.
- Connects to the standard telephone service and is therefore simple to locate.
- Facilities for automation enable documents to be transmitted at designated times to take advantage of cheaper telephone rates.
- Faxes do not need a human presence to receive documents.
- Electronically stored documents can be transmitted directly to a fax machine where facilities are installed in the electronic communications system.

There are number of things you can do to ensure that your use of these facilities are effective and trouble-free:

- A cover sheet, indicating the source, destination, subject and number of pages, can greatly aid the process of getting the document to the right person.
- Only use good quality documents in the fax machine – you may need to make a photocopy if the document is not clear, on the right size of paper or damaged.
- Make sure that the margins are sufficient as the information at the edges may distort.
- Check received documents to ensure all the pages have been received and are legible.
- If the fax received is not for you, pass it on quickly as this method of document transmission is usually used because the document is needed urgently.
- When using a fax/phone, you will need to change the settings to fax to be able to send or receive documents.

CHECK IT YOURSELF

What fax facilities do you have access to? Is it a dedicated fax machine or computer-based fax facilities and, if so, what software do you use? Do you have a standard front cover? Complete section 1 of the electronic communication checklist on p. 154. You will need to include this in your evidence folder as supplementary evidence.

Network communications

Many activities carried out on a computer on a day-to-day basis are only needed in the immediate work environment and might use the computer in a stand-alone mode, but there are many reasons why the computers in an organisation may be part of a computer network.

Local area networks (LANs) exist where computers are located within relatively short distances of one another, usually within the same building. These are often necessary as people within the organisation need to share information and communicate with each other electronically.

When working in a network environment it is possible to:

- share data files
- share software
- share resources such as printers and high-capacity storage devices
- work from a number of different locations
- use messaging systems including e-mail.

Network topologies

The topology of a network describes the physical organisation of the network in terms of how it is wired together. There are several different methods each with their advantages and disadvantages.

Star network

Each workstation is connected to the main, central resource (file server) by means of its own cabling. The significant advantage of this method is its speed as data from only one computer is travelling down the line. It is also reasonably secure as no workstation can communicate directly with another without going through the central resource. The main disadvantage is that if a link is severed, then the workstation becomes disconnected as there is no other route through.

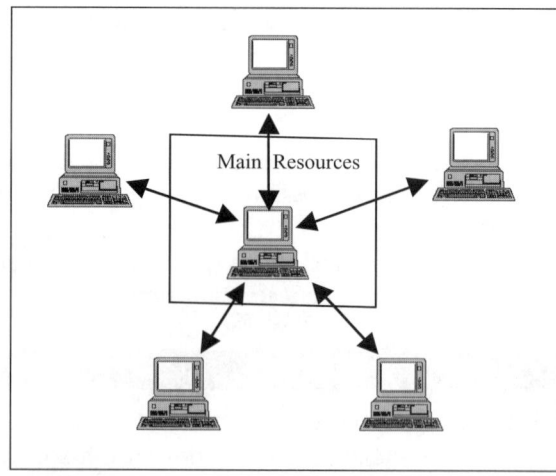

Figure 32 *A star network*

Ring network

All the workstations and the main resources are cabled in a complete ring. One of the first types was the Cambridge ring, developed at Cambridge University. A workstation will initiate a message, a packet of data, which gets sent to the next workstation along the line. If it is intended for this workstation it is received; if it is not then it is boosted by a repeater and sent to the workstation. This continues until it reaches the station it is intended for.

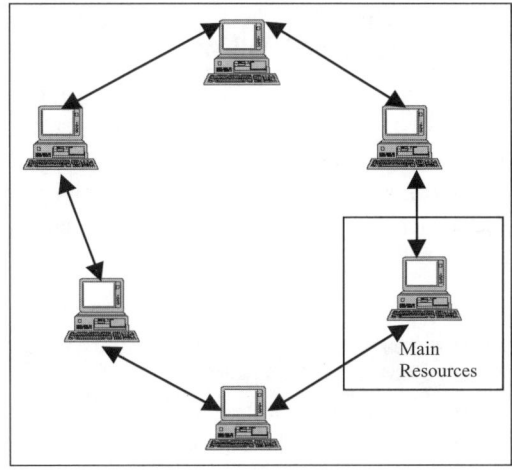

Figure 33 *A ring network*

An improvement to this is the token ring system where an electronic token passes continuously around the network. When a workstation needs to communicate, it grabs the token and sends its data packet. This system avoids clashes of packets of data and, although it may sound slow, it only really becomes an issue with a very heavily used network.

Bus network

In a bus network there is a common cable which usually has a terminator at each end. The workstations are on spurs along the common cable. One of the workstations along the cable provides the main resources, the file server. This type of network is generally cheaper to install than a star network but is far less secure as the data packets can be intercepted from any workstation. If the network is very heavily used then, as all the users share the same cabling, the response times will be slow unless there is sufficient bandwidth.

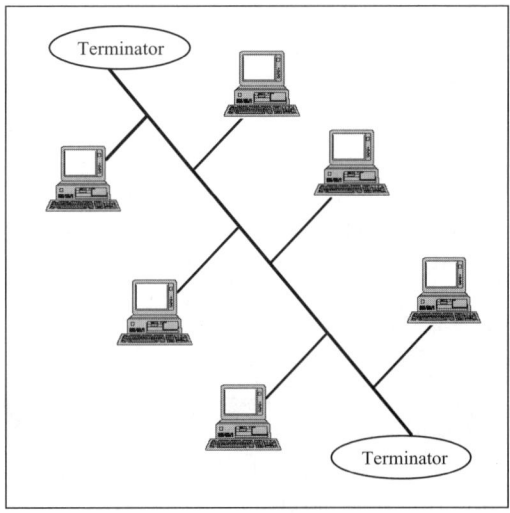

Figure 34 *A bus network*

However, with a bus network using hubs, and a star topology at each spur, this becomes a more reliable and responsive network.

Similar networks are also frequently established using telecommunications systems, so that communication and sharing of resources can take place over a wider area (WANs). These networks are not limited to the same physical restrictions as a LAN. The LAN topologies are, however, not appropriate and a mesh network will exist, where potentially any computer can connect to any other on the network.

CHECK IT YOURSELF

What network facilities do you have access to? What network topology is used? What is the name and version of the network software? Complete section 2 of the electronic communication checklist on p. 154. You will need to include this in your evidence folder as supplementary evidence.

Electronic mail

Electronic mail, more usually referred to as e-mail, is an electronic communication system that enables users to send messages and information to a recipient's mail-box and to retrieve messages and information from their own mail-box. It is a means of carrying out rapid, reliable and recorded communication both within an organisation and externally. In many organisations, the use of e-mail has replaced completely the use of memos and sometimes even letters.

To be able to use e-mail your computer will need to be connected to a network (internal or external) and have the appropriate e-mail software on the system. The e-mail system, like any other system, needs to be managed and supported. There will usually be a post-master who has responsibility for setting up each mailbox, maintaining global mailing lists and other network-wide services.

CHECK IT YOURSELF

What e-mail facilities do you have access to? Does it include both internal and external e-mail? What software do you use to access it? Enter this information in section 3 of the electronic communication checklist on p. 154. You will need to include this in your evidence folder as supplementary evidence.

You will need to be able to use all the main features of the e-mail facilities. As well as using the basic functions of e-mail, that is to send and receive mail, you will need to use a range of other functions including the following:

- The reply facility of the system will enable you to handle your mail more speedily, as the name and e-mail address of the sender are already in the system. Likewise, you can forward any message to a third party, without the need to re-create it.

- You can set priorities for your messages, indicating that it has an urgent, standard or low priority. If you need to know that your message has been received and read, you can set it so that you will be automatically sent a receipt when it arrives and when it is read.

- When you word process a memo, you spell check it and proof read it, but very few people do this as standard with their e-mails and yet frequently they are as important. Most e-mail software will have a spell checker available and you should be able to configure it so that it will run automatically when you click on the 'send' button, thus avoiding poorly spelled documents.

- You can keep your own address book of e-mail addresses. You can add, edit and delete these addresses and can quickly access them when addressing a message. You can change the settings of your software so that when you receive mail from a new address, it is automatically added to your address book. In most organisations you will have access to a centrally maintained (global) address book with all the internal users' addresses that will be maintained by the organisations' post-master, as well as your own address book which you maintain.

- When you need to communicate regularly with a group of people, a mailing list can be set up with all their addresses. This speeds up the process of creating these messages and ensures that individuals are not accidentally omitted. In many instances mailing lists for groups within the organisation, for example the board of directors, will be set up and maintained centrally by the post-master.

- You can attach documents and other electronic files to an e-mail message. There may be restrictions set by the post-master as to the types of files that can be attached and also limits on the size of the file. These restrictions are usually imposed for security reasons and to reduce the volume of the traffic on the system which can adversely affect its speed. There may be occasions when you will need to compress files, using an appropriate utility, to comply with these regulations.

- There may be occasions when you want your e-mail to be handled automatically. You can set the system so that mail can be organised directly into specific folders based on the address of the sender, or you may wish to set up an automatic reply to indicate that you will not be available to deal with your mail for a period of time. You can also re-direct your mail to another e-mail address where it can be dealt with.

Mail-boxes, just like any other mail and storage system, need to be managed. Most e-mail systems are set up to keep all the messages received in an 'inbox', the messages sent in a 'sent' folder, any messages that have been written but not yet sent in an 'outbox' and all the deleted messages in a 'deleted' folder. In time, the storage taken up by the e-mail system can be quite significant, particularly in a large organisation.

In a business environment, many of the e-mails will carry the same status as a memo or letter and therefore a record needs to be kept. It is important to note that e-mails now have the same legal standing as other, more traditional forms of communication. There are few advantages in printing out most of these messages, and so you need to set up an appropriate electronic storage system. There will, of course, be messages that you do not need to keep and these should be deleted.

There will usually be a set of standard procedures laid down by the organisation as to how the e-mails are structured, which will usually include specific guidelines about signatures. Your e-mail software can be set up with a default signature and you can set it up so that you can select different signatures for different recipients. Many organisations' e-mails carry a standard statement about the content of the e-mail and how to handle e-mails that have been incorrectly received, as shown in the example below.

****

The information in this internet eMail is confidential and is intended solely for the addressee(s). Access, copying, dissemination or re-use of information in it by anyone else is unauthorised. Any views or opinions presented are solely those of the author and do not necessarily represent those of Autoware.

If you are not the intended recipient please contact

Autoware, Newbury, +44(0)1234 56789

Figure 35 *An e-mail disclaimer*

CHECK IT YOURSELF

The electronic communication checklist on p. 154 includes all the main e-mail features you need to be able to use in your particular software. As you progress through the qualification, add this information to section 3 so that you can include this in your evidence folder as supplementary evidence.

E-mails, security and the law

The ease with which most individuals can access e-mail systems raises issues of security. High risk or confidential information can very easily be distributed across such a system. All users need to be aware of this and, in particular, the immediacy of e-mail. If I put a piece of paper in an envelope for the post, there are many stages along the way when I could possibly intercept it, but with e-mail once the send button is pressed there is little I can do. In addition to this, one of the main sources of computer viruses nowadays is from external e-mail systems. Great care should be taken when reading unsolicited mail from an unknown source, and particularly when opening attachments.

A number of legal cases recently have helped to give e-mail the same legal status as paper-based documentation. E-mails are subject to the same libel, privacy and obscenity laws as paper-based communications. The Regulation of Investigatory Powers (RIP) Act puts e-mail on the same standing as telephone calls and letters allowing the interception of e-mail by government. Corporations can monitor employees' e-mail as long as they have stated their plans to do so.

The Internet

The Internet is a network of networks all working under the same *protocol* (set of rules) to communicate. The connection to the Internet will be made available by an Internet Provider (IP) and the system will be using the standard rules and procedures for connection – TCP/IP (Transmission Control Protocol/Internet Protocol).

There are a number of different facilities available on the Internet. The one you are probably most familiar with is the World Wide Web (www). This is a graphical user interface (GUI) to access the resources on the Internet. Using HTML (hypertext mark-up language), pages are set up and contain links to other pages and sites to enable the user to 'surf the net'.

To access the World Wide Web you need to have a browser. This is software that can read the HTML code and will enable you to navigate the web, moving around the pages to access information, download images and text and to print pages where appropriate.

The information on the Internet is not organised, nor is it controlled or managed in any way other than by the individual website managers. Therefore, to be able to search effectively across this network of information you will often need to use one of the many search engines that are available. These are interactive services which have access to vast catalogues of hundreds of thousands of websites which can be found through key word searches. There is an ever-increasing number of such tools available and some of the more sophisticated 'learn' through responses to searches so that they can improve their search results.

FTP (File Transfer Protocol) is a standard that enables you to transmit files across the Internet. This method is used by many organisations as a means of transferring data to other users and also a way of giving their employees access to files whilst away from the place of work.

The Internet is now a standard business tool. Most organisations will have a website which, at the very least, will provide a view into the organisation and its core business. For many organisations this will be little more than an electronic brochure publicising their activities and products or services. However, for many organisations, e-commerce is becoming an additional if not alternative method of operation and many companies now offer their customers opportunities to carry out business transactions, such as ordering of goods or services, over the web.

CHECK IT YOURSELF

What Internet facilities do you have access to, who is the Internet Provider and how is the connection made? What is the name of the browser you usually use and the search engines you use most frequently? Do you use the Internet for any aspects of e-commerce, and if so what? Complete section 4 of the electronic communication checklist on p. 154. You will need to include this in your evidence folder as supplementary evidence.

Intranets and extranets

An intranet is a web browser-based network that is only available from within the organisation. Many businesses now provide access to the organisation's information systems in this way as this environment is 'user friendly' and familiar to most people. The development tools to produce such an interface are relatively cheap and the development process, except for complex database applications, is usually quite straightforward.

Easy-to-use query facilities will be included, often resembling the search tools of proprietary search engines, to enable users to make full use of the services and, with well-designed links, the user can navigate the system with ease.

CHECK IT YOURSELF

Do you have access to an intranet and what do you use it for? How do find information on this service; is there a search facility? Complete section 5 of the electronic communication checklist on p. 155. You will need to include this in your evidence folder as supplementary evidence.

An extratnet is the name used to describe an organisations' web browser-based network that is available to external users such as customers and suppliers. With an extranet comes quick communication with customers and other specified users enabling the organisation to be more responsive and often improve effectiveness of its operations.

The use of web technology has provided freedom from specific platforms. As the applications software uses a web-based interface it means that not only is it readily available to all who need it, but also it solves the software development and support problems that exist with the traditional applications software approach.

With intranets, and more particularly extranets, protection against unwanted intrusion is necessary. This will be achieved through the use of a firewall. A firewall is a system or group of systems that enforces an access control between two networks. The firewall will either permit traffic between the networks or block traffic. The firewall will need to be configured with the access control policy of the organisation, indicating what traffic is permitted and what not. Because a firewall keeps a log of all attempts to access the network, legitimate or otherwise, it can provide a valuable auditing tool with summary information about the security of your network.

CHECK IT YOURSELF

Do you have access to an extranet and what do you use it for? How do find information on this service; is there a search facility? What firewalls exist to protect it from unlawful access? Add this information to section 5 of the electronic communication checklist on p. 155. You will need to include this in your evidence folder as supplementary evidence.

Electronic communication checklist

Section 1: fax	
dedicated fax machine?	
computer-based fax?	
software used	
standard front cover available?	
Section 2: network facilities	
topology	
network software	
software version	
Section 3: e-mail	
e-mail service provider	
e-mail software	
post-master	
read	
reply	
forward	
spell check	
local address book	
global address book	
mailing lists	
auto responder	
file attachments – including compression	
e-mail filing system	
Section 4: Internet	
Internet Provider	
method of connection	
search engine used	
browser	
e-commerce?	

Electronic communication checklist (continued)

Section 5: Intranet and extranet	
is there an intranet?	
is there a query language?	
do you access an extranet?	
is there a firewall?	

Case Study Activity

Information about the company Autoware has been included in the form of a case study on pp. 157–62. It describes the nature and structure of the organisation and will provide you with a context in which to carry out this task. It is therefore essential that you read this before you attempt this activity.

Autoware uses electronic systems for much of its communications, both within the organisation and externally. Whilst this has many advantages for the speed at which they can operate, there are many issues attached to these methods. The need to organise and manage e-mail is something that most organisations have not fully appreciated, and the many legal implications need to be acknowledged.

1. Carry out some research into how other organisations have attempted to manage this. You will need to find out all the issues relating to the legal status of this method of communication and the impact this will have on the company. The Internet will be a good source for some of this information.

2. You now need to create a set of guidelines for employees on working with e-mail. It should include:

   - 'netiquette'
   - standard information
   - personal e-mail
   - monitoring
   - file storage and archiving
   - auto responders, redirection, etc.

Case study Autoware

Autoware is a specialist software house. The primary business of the company is to design and support computer systems for sales and service within the automotive trade. These systems have been developed over a considerable number of years and are used by hundreds of motor traders all over the country, and also in many European countries. The company has built up a vast level of expertise in this area of work and is now one of the main suppliers of such systems in the UK.

The structure of the organisation

There are development, support, marketing, sales and finance departments within the organisation, each supported by administrative staff. Each department is headed by a senior manager who, with the Managing Director and Chief Executive, make up the board of directors. A management information systems (MIS) department operates to provide computing services across the organisation which is managed by the Finance Director.

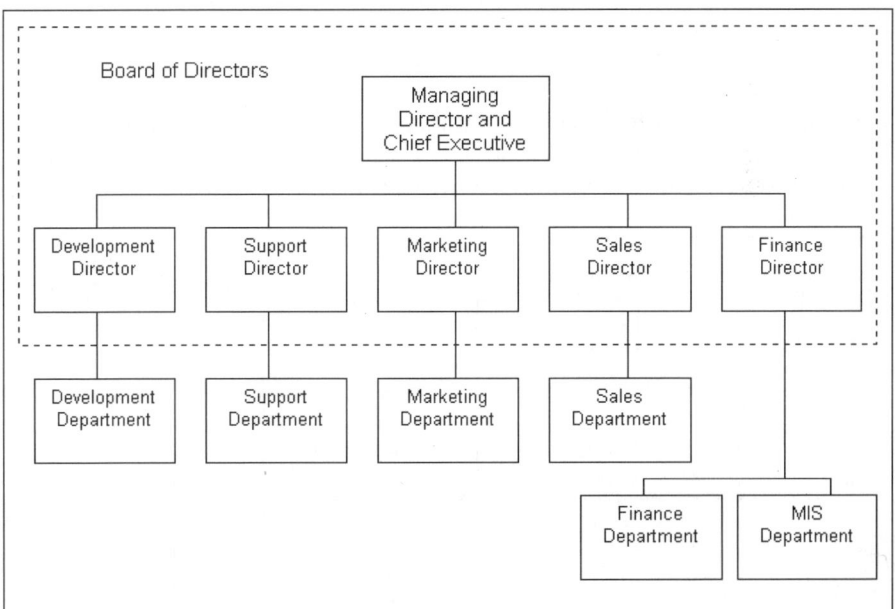

Figure 36   *An organisation chart*

The organisation of each of the departments varies to meet the different needs.

The **development department** consists of two teams of staff, each headed by a team manager. The design team works on new designs and modifications to existing designs and the maintenance team carries out any software development work necessary to fix or keep the existing systems working.

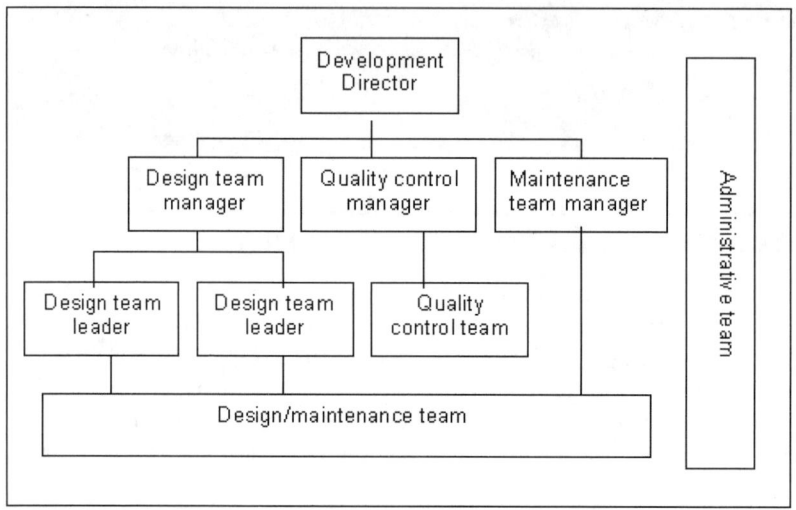

Figure 37   *Development department*

The **support team** consists of technical support consultants who are available to provide on-site support and a team of online support personnel who provide telephone advice and assistance.

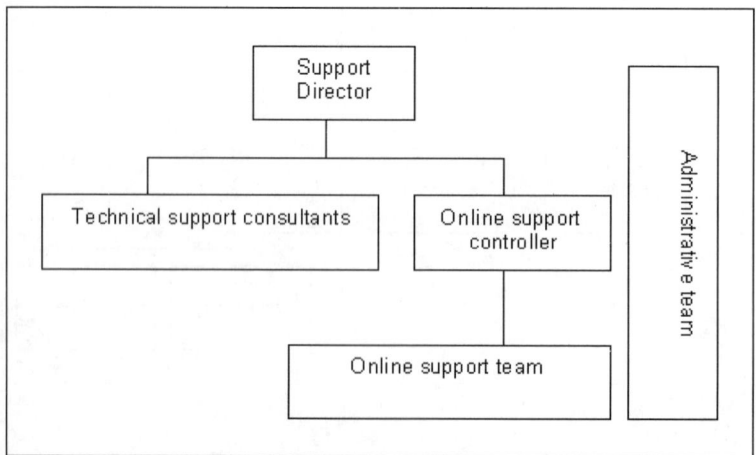

Figure 38   *Support team*

The **marketing department** consists of the web master, an advertising team and an information team who write most of the user manuals and leaflets.

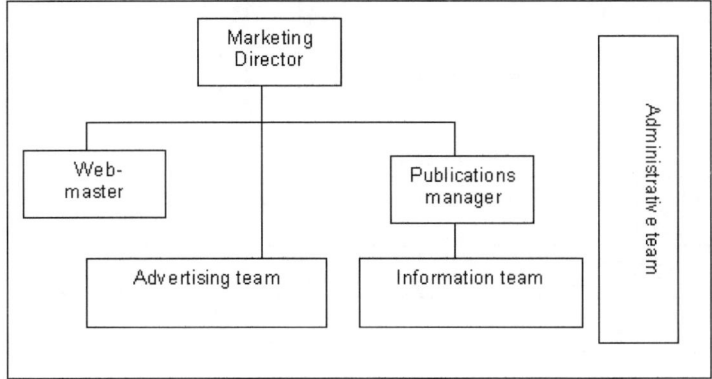

Figure 39 *Marketing department*

The **sales department** processes orders for new customers and maintains the database of licence maintenance contracts.

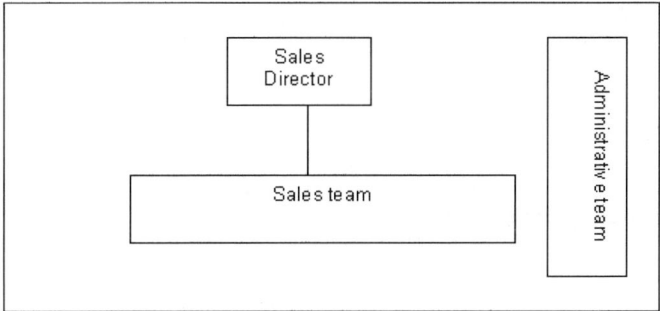

Figure 40 *Sales department*

The **finance department** maintains the financial records of the company, processing all invoices and recording customer credit details.

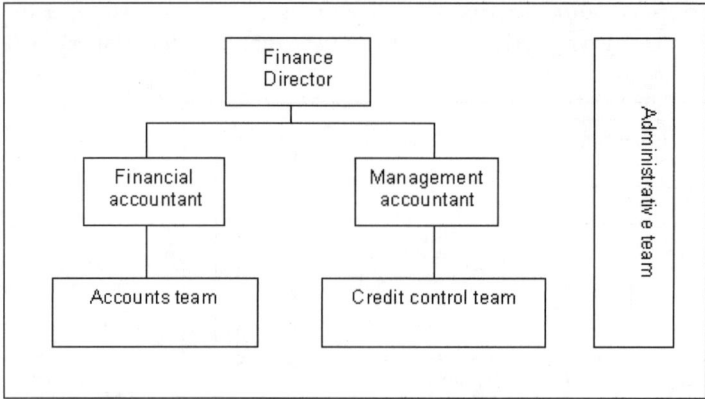

Figure 41 *Finance department*

The **MIS** department provides computing services across the organisation, and particularly to support the business operations of the organisation.

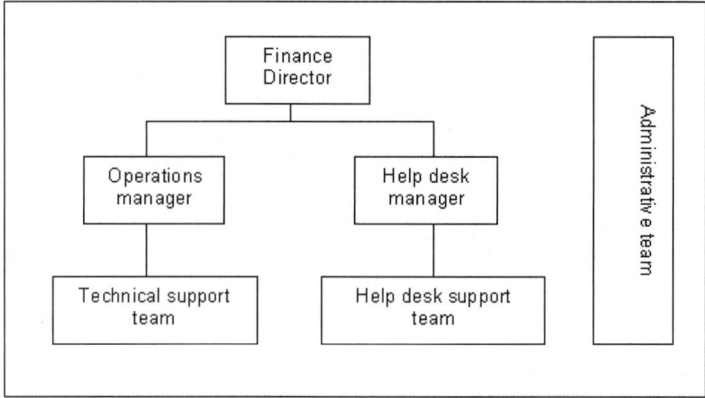

Figure 42 *MIS department*

The flow of information through the organisation

To have a good understanding of how the organisation operates, you need to know about the flow of information throughout the organisation.

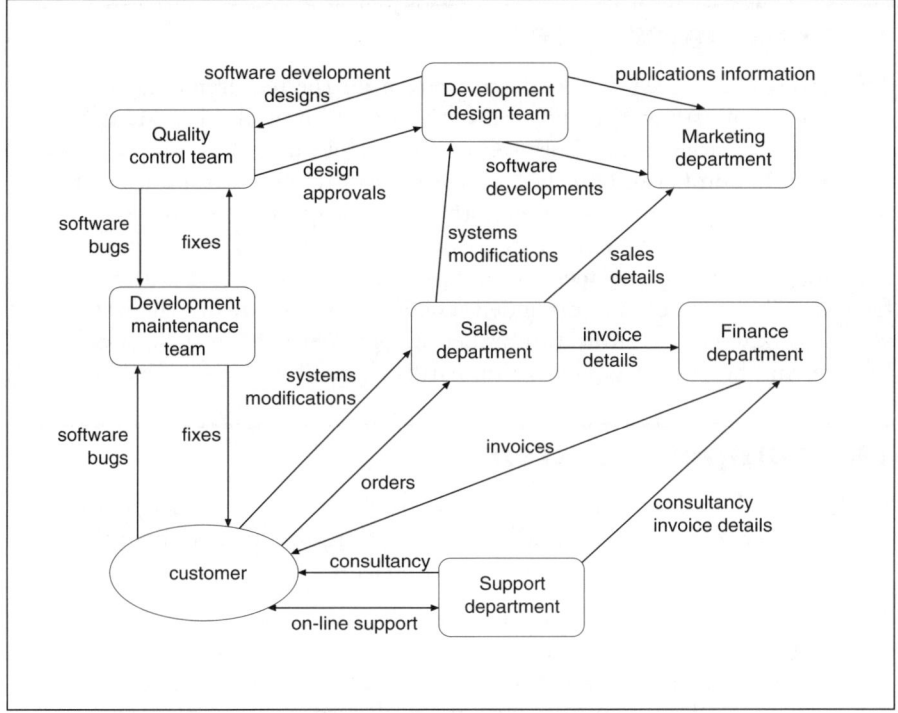

Figure 43 *The flow of information in an organisation*

A new customer purchases a licence to use the system. This licence will be for a specified number of users and is priced accordingly. There is a one-off licence fee at the time of purchase and the customer will then pay an annual maintenance charge, again based upon the number of users licensed.

Amendments to the systems may be instigated at the suggestion of a customer, through the sales team, or from within the development team. All software development must be approved by quality control at all stages of the development.

Software bugs will be monitored by quality control and may be notified by customers, software development or the support team. They will be prioritised on the basis of their impact on the continuing satisfactory operation of the systems and other planned developments.

Users will receive unlimited online and telephone support as part of their maintenance agreement together with any upgrades and new releases of the software. They may also request consultancy support for which they will pay additional fees.

All administrative aspects of the organisation are computerised, with e-mail as the primary method of communication, both internally and with customers around the world.

The customer base

The systems have been designed and written for the requirements of the automotive industry – this includes both cars and motorcycles. Many of the customers are large national or even international car dealers with a considerable number of branches. However, Autoware also supplies systems to much smaller businesses; to meet the needs of the very small business, it supplies a 'cut-down' release of the main systems. This has all of the main system functionality but does not provide multi-site communications features. The company has expanded its customer base within the last five years and now has a significant number of customer sites in the rest of Europe, and has recently moved into parts of Asia.

The computer systems

As one would expect with a software company, all aspects of its operations are computerised. However, systems and their requirements frequently change and these therefore need regular updating.

All parts of the offices are cabled for the extensive network system so that any changes in the use of the buildings will not be inhibited by access to the technology. All staff have access to PCs connected to the network, and most development staff have laptops, with network cards, as they may need to take these to the customer's site.

Internet connection is available at all points. Autoware has an extensive website which is mainly directed at marketing and providing update information to existing customers. An intranet is used to enable information to be readily shared; this is particularly important in a development environment where problems and solutions need to be immediately available to everyone.

Appendix Jobs in ICT

The recruitment and selection process

Organisations recruit staff for a variety of reasons:

- Filling vacancies arising from resignations, retirements and dismissals.
  There will be a turnover of staff in most organisations. People will leave
  to go to other jobs because there are different or better opportunities, or
  because they need to move and are too far away to continue to travel.
  Others will leave the organisation as they reach retirement age,
  sometimes gradually reducing their work commitment with a 'hand
  over' period so that they can train their replacement. There may also be
  occasions where an organisation dismisses an employee.
- Internal promotions. There may be occasions when a member of staff is
  promoted within the organisation and his or her existing post will
  become vacant.
- Growth of the organisation. New posts may arise in an organisation
  brought about by expansion and a growth in resources.
- Changing job roles within the organisation. Where the nature or
  structure of the organisation changes, new or different posts may need to
  be filled to support the changing ways of working.

An organisation will often use the opportunity presented by a vacancy to
review the post, to ascertain whether it is still required, and to ensure that
the roles and responsibilities are still appropriate.

Recruitment can be a time consuming and costly process and it is therefore
essential to use methods and procedures that are likely to result in
appropriate selection and appointment of personnel.

Selection methods and procedures

Preparation of job description and personal specification

Job descriptions can take many forms. Many organisations will have a
generic job description for similar jobs at the same level, any variations
being identified in the letter of appointment or as an addition to the job
description. A job description will include the title of the job, the identity
of the line manager and also any staff management responsibilities of the
post. It will describe the duties of the post and may also include details of
location, level and remuneration.

In addition many organisations will create a personal specification. This
describes the skills, knowledge and experience required to do the job. It will

usually identify those that are essential and those that are desirable. It can provide a very useful reference for any applicant, who can make sure that he or she is applying for the right job and can address all aspects of this personal specification in the application. It will then also be used by the organisation to identify suitable candidates.

Careful planning of how, where and when to advertise

There are many options available to an organisation as to how to advertise a post. Jobs can be advertised in newspapers and magazines; this could be a local paper, a national paper or a specialist publication. Jobs can also be advertised through a recruitment agency; here the agency will decide how to make information about the job known to prospective candidates. It will have registered clients on its books, but may also advertise in publications, etc. Many jobs are now advertised on the Internet. There are Internet-based employment agencies and many organisations advertise vacancies on their own websites.

The nature of the job, the organisation and its recruitment policy will influence these decisions. You will need to be aware of the possible places for the type of job you are looking for, and search all the possible sources.

The time period from the decision to recruit to an appointment being made can be quite considerable. The organisation will need to take this into consideration when placing an advertisement. It will need to indicate a closing date for the applications, and this will need to reflect the urgency of the appointment and the availability of relevant personnel who need to take part in the process.

Shortlisting of candidates

The applications, in whatever form, will be examined to identify potentially suitable candidates. This process is known as shortlisting. Employers identify candidates' strengths and weakness based on the contents of the job application forms, curriculum vitae and letters of application. It is therefore absolutely essential that you provide a complete picture of yourself to give you the best chance possible to be shortlisted.

Making an application

The CV

CV stands for curriculum vitae. It is the main document you can use to describe yourself to a prospective employer. It contains details about your personal background, your aspirations and ambitions, your work experience, your skills and knowledge, your education, and other relevant activities.

It is important to remember that, just as your career and experiences develop, so your CV also needs to be developed. It needs to be kept current and relevant to the direction in which you intend to progress. It therefore makes sense to set it up as a word processed document that you can amend and re-arrange whenever you need to. With the high-level of word processing and presentation skills that you will have developed while working towards this qualification, you should be able to produce a professional and well-presented document. This will not only enable you to describe yourself but will also give you the opportunity to demonstrate your IT and presentation skills to any prospective employer.

The layout and content of your CV will need to be varied according to its purpose. You will usually find that you will need to amend its emphasis to meet the specific requirements of the job you are applying for. It will need to be more comprehensive if it is to be submitted as the main document, together with a letter of application (see below), rather than if it is accompanying an application form. It is also useful to have an outline CV which just contains the basic facts – dates, addresses, etc. – so that you can refer to it when completing any forms.

CV layout

The style and presentation of CVs have changed over the years. This has to some extent been influenced by the technology available to produce the final document.

When creating a CV, you need to take into account the intended recipient of the information. As this is a document that you want to be read in full, it must not be too long (usually not longer than two pages), and it must be relevant. It needs to have a clear presentation and be organised so that the reader can quickly gain an impression of you, your knowledge, expertise and skills and can easily find the information he or she is looking for. It is usual to organise your CV into discrete sections, including an appropriate heading for each. Your CV needs to include sections for personal details, career history, relevant skills and expertise, education, training, interests and hobbies, and references. As an introduction, it is quite common to include a brief summary or profile of yourself, highlighting your most relevant achievements, experience and skills. You might also include a section describing your personal objectives, giving details of your aspirations and goals.

Personal details

Personal details will need to include:

- name – if you have changed your name you should indicate this, particularly if some of your qualifications are in a different name or your referees know you by another name
- title – you might want to include this, especially if you wish to be addressed in a particular way such as Ms rather than Mrs or Miss, or Dr, etc.

- date of birth – most prospective employers will require this information
- address – obviously, a prospective employer needs to have an address, and usually also telephone number and even an e-mail address, at which to contact you.

There may be additional basic information that you wish to include here such as your National Insurance number, work permit details, etc.

CHECK IT YOURSELF

Complete section 1 of the CV information sheet on p. 182 with all your personal details. Add any additional information you consider relevant in the 'other' box.

Career history

Career history is the section that provides details of each organisation for which you have worked, including unpaid work. It should be presented in chronological order, starting with the most recent. You would usually include the name and address of the organisation, the dates you were working there (month and year), the title of the job you held, a brief description of the post identifying your duties and responsibilities, and the salary or wages you received and/or job grade if relevant. You should highlight your achievements in the post. Long paragraphs of text will not get read, so make sure the information is concise and relevant.

It is extremely important that all your time is accounted for, including non-paid or voluntary work and any time dedicated to parental or other care duties.

CHECK IT YOURSELF

Complete Section 2 of the CV information sheet on p. 182 with details of your career history.

Relevant skills and knowledge

Relevant skills and knowledge is the section where you can identify the skills and expertise you have that are particularly relevant to the type of work you are seeking. You need to include the high-level IT skills you have, specifying the exact packages and hardware you can use and indicating some of the ways in which you have used them. You will also need to identify the staff supervision, training and support expertise you have, again giving specific examples.

Complete section 3 of the CV information sheet on p. 183 with details of all the skills and knowledge you have that would be of interest to a prospective employer.

Education and training

Education and training needs to provide information about your education from age 11. This should include each school, college or other training organisation you have attended, and it should be in chronological order. You should give the name and address of the institution, the dates you attended, the subjects studied and the qualifications gained. If you attended part time, this information should also be given.

As well as formal education, you should include details about relevant training courses you have attended, particularly recent activities you have been involved in.

Complete section 4 of the CV information sheet on p. 183 with details of your education and training and any training courses you have attended.

Interests and hobbies

Most employers are interested to know a little about their prospective employees in terms of what they do or are interested in outside of work. This is where your personality can come across in your CV. Employers are particularly interested in any interests and activities that show leadership skills (eg parent governor at your child's primary school) and teamwork expertise (eg member of local cricket team) or ones that involve accepting responsibility (eg treasurer for a local playgroup).

Complete section 5 of the CV information sheet on p. 183 with information about your interests, hobbies and other activities.

References

Employers will usually want to contact two people who can confirm your suitability for employment, and the job under consideration in particular. They will need the referee's name and his or her relationship to you (eg manager, tutor, etc.). Your referees will need to be able to supply information about your suitability for employment in terms of your attitude to work, your enthusiasms, commitment and level of skills. They will also need to be able to confirm your experience, qualifications and knowledge. The employer will want to know that you are reliable, honest and professional in the way you work. For some jobs, employers will be particularly concerned with confirming specific aspects of the job; for example, if the job requires working with the general public they may be concerned with the level and quality of your communications and interpersonal skills, or if the job involves handling money, they would need to know that you were trustworthy. Remember to gain the permission of your referees *before* giving their details on an application.

CHECK IT YOURSELF

Complete section 6 of the CV information sheet on p. 183 with details of two people you could ask to act as referees.

Personal objectives

You should also include a personal objectives section in which you need to demonstrate that this is the area of work appropriate for you. You will need to include a statement about how you wish your career to develop, and ensure that this relates to the opportunities in the job you are applying for.

CHECK IT YOURSELF

What are your job or career plans? What sort of job are you looking for now, and what sort of work would you like to be doing in five years' time? Write a few clear sentences outlining both your short- and medium-term ambitions. Make sure they are realistic and draw upon the skills, knowledge and experience you are gaining on this qualification. At this stage, unless you are applying for a specific job, this will probably need to be a fairly general statement and, remember, it will need to be revised each time you use it so that it relates to the specific post you are applying for.

Summary or profile

Although you should place the summary or profile near the beginning of the CV, you really need to write it when you have completed all the other sections of the CV. This summary will form some of the first impressions that prospective employers have about you. It will therefore need to give the information that will make them want to read the rest of the CV.

Final points on preparing a CV

It is important to make sure that your CV accounts for all your time from your secondary education onwards. If you had some time out after school before going to college or embarking on your career (eg a gap year), indicate this and say what you did during this time, whether travelling, gaining skills or doing voluntary work etc. If you have had time out as a carer (of children or sick/elderly relatives), include this information.

If you have access to the Internet, there are several websites that provide information on how to create a CV. Some of these offer a range of CV writing services which you will have to pay for, but others offer free advice and guidance on how to create your own. Do be aware where the site is based as the expectations of CVs in America are quite different from those in the UK.

An example of a CV is given on pp. 179–80.

Filling in a form

Many organisations will require you to complete an application form. In many instances they may specifically state that you should *not* include a CV, or that a CV may be included but the form must still be completed in full. The questions in application forms can vary quite considerably. Much of the form will ask for basic details about yourself, your previous work experience and education, and qualifications you have gained. If you have prepared an outline CV, most of this is simply a matter of transferring the information to the form. There will also be a section (often little more than a blank page) where you are asked to write about why and how you are particularly suitable for the job. This is almost always the most important part of the form, and where you need to concentrate your efforts. In this section you should include information from your CV such as the summary, personal objectives, skills and knowledge, and relevant experience. Make sure you focus on those aspects of your experience that are particularly relevant to the job you are applying for. If there is a personal specification, this is where you should make sure that every requirement is specifically addressed. Sometimes this is best achieved by organising this section into headings, one for each requirement.

Make sure that you first read any guidance about how the form is to be completed. It may specify that the form must be filled in with black ink – this is usually to ensure that good quality photocopies can be made – or it may require that it is hand written. Some employers engage specialists to analyse your handwriting to gain an insight into your personality, temperament and suitability for the job.

If you are applying electronically, you may be asked to complete an electronic application. This will be very similar to filling in a paper-based form, but be careful – if you have completed the form online, you should check it very thoroughly on screen before you send it; once the send or OK button is pressed, it has been sent and cannot be stopped.

Writing a letter

A letter of application will usually be required where there is no application form. Its purpose is to introduce you and your CV and to make clear which job you are applying for. You need to clearly highlight the specific skills, knowledge and experience that you have which make you particularly suitable for the position. It is usually appropriate to make reference to recent work experience and identify any training which is particularly relevant, but don't just repeat the whole of your CV. Don't make the letter too long – it needs to be clear, brief and very much to the point. You want the reader to be interested enough to look through your CV. An example of a letter of application is shown on p. 181.

When making an application in this way, you will need to ensure that your CV is comprehensive and supplies sufficient detail about yourself and why you should be considered for the job in question. You will need to ensure that, where a personal specification is provided, that all the required elements are covered either in the CV or in the letter of application, and that the essential ones are highlighted in the letter.

Research

When applying for a job, you need to find out as much as you can about the organisation. You may well have been sent information from the organisation such as a glossy brochure, the annual report, or information especially prepared for candidates. You should also do some research of your own, and the obvious starting point is to check if the organisation a website; many organisations both large and small have their own site. This will give you information about the organisation and how it presents itself, and should enable you to get a 'feel' about it.

You should also do some research about the sector in which the organisation is based, eg financial services, housing, publishing, etc. This should give you some insight into the nature of the organisation, how it might operate and current issues it may be concerned with. This research should help you to prepare for the interview and suggest some pertinent questions to ask at the interview.

The recruitment interview

Planning

Every organisation has its own views on how best to select candidates for a job. It is therefore a good idea, wherever possible, to find out beforehand what is going to take place. Many organisations will give some indication of this in the invitation for interview. Interviews need to be planned and both interviewer and interviewee need to prepare in advance.

The interview process will often involve two stages. First interviews tend to be on a one-to-one basis with either your prospective line manager or the personnel manager, or a panel interview where you meet several people either jointly or individually. In many organisations, there will be a clear set of guidelines about the questions to be asked at interview. The panel of interviewers will meet beforehand to agree the questions to be asked to ensure that all aspects of the personal specification are covered. Most organisations will then invite shortlisted candidates back for a second or final interview. Often at this stage you would be able to meet other members of the team and see the working environment.

As the candidate, you will also need to prepare for the interview. You will need to make sure that you are fully aware of the requirements for the job and how you are able to meet them. It is a good idea to keep a copy of the information you have supplied so that you can review it before the interview. Check through the job description and personal specification to make sure you can demonstrate that you have the required skills, knowledge and experience. Try and identify at least one example for each of the requirements for the job and remember, they do not all need to be taken from paid employment or in the field of IT; they could be for tasks you have carried out in a voluntary capacity, supervision of volunteers in a playgroup, etc.

Make sure you have a map of where you are going to and have planned exactly how to get there. Take into account potential delays such as traffic jams and train cancellations when deciding on how much time to allow to for the journey. You do not want to arrive too early and have to 'kill' time, if you are 'just in time' you will not have time to collect your thoughts, and if you arrive late you will seriously reduce your chances of being considered for the post.

Interviewer techniques

The interviewer needs to provide the candidate with the opportunity to demonstrate his or her suitability for the post. To do this, it is essential to create the right environment; the candidate needs to be able to feel at ease and comfortable enough to be able to give his or her best. Interview questions need to be directed to the candidate in such a way as to offer him or her the opportunity to demonstrate skills and knowledge. The majority of questions need to be of an *open* nature, to give the candidate the opportunity to respond as he or she sees fit, rather than using *closed* questions which restrict the candidate's scope.

The interviewer will need to keep a record of what takes place in the interview. Sometimes a member of staff from the personnel department provides this service, thus freeing up the interviewer to concentrate on the actual interview. There may be some form of checklist, relating to the personal specification, which is used to confirm the extent to which each one is met.

Interviewee techniques

You, the interviewee, need to make sure you are as well prepared as possible to be able to be comfortable during the actual interview. Bring all the information you have about the job with you. Also have readily available all the key information about yourself, as it is all too easy to get flustered and confused in a high pressure situation.

You need to make a good impression during the interview, not just regarding your knowledge and expertise but also as someone the organisation would like to have around. You need to be confident and polite, smile – but not inappropriately. Make frequent eye contact with the interviewer, and in a panel interview, it is important to include all the members of the panel in your answers and not just the individual who asked the question. Take your time when answering questions, and ask for clarification if you are not sure you have understood what is required. Make sure that you are answering the question asked and keep to the point. Your answers will need to be factual and complete, and avoid simple 'yes' or 'no' answers as these do not give very much information and therefore do not 'sell' you to the interviewer. It is usually a good idea to illustrate your answers with practical examples (see **planning**), but make sure they are relevant.

Try to be honest in your responses, but not blunt. If you are negative in the way you react you are less likely to be successful. For example, when discussing your present employment, a response of "I enjoy my present job but, as there are very limited opportunities to progress in the direction I would like to go" is a better reply the "I am bored with the work I am currently doing and do not feel appreciated".

You will usually be given the opportunity to ask questions at the end of the interview. This is your chance to clarify any aspects of the job or the way the organisation operates. You can use this time to demonstrate your interest in the job, possibly drawing upon the information gained in your research.

A mock interview can be extremely useful, particularly if it is a long time since you had an interview. Ideally, it should be conducted in as similar a situation as possible to a 'real' interview. There are organisations that will provide this kind of help; for example, 'job clubs' will usually offer this type of service. It is essential that you get constructive feedback after the interview, so that you are aware of your strengths and weaknesses in this type of situation.

Evaluation and decisions

The interviewers will usually meet soon after the completion of the interview process to discuss the merits of each of the candidates. If this does not take place immediately after the interviews, it is extremely important that accurate records are available to support the process. Where there is a personal specification, the extent to which each candidate meets the requirements will be agreed. Where there is more than one candidate that meets all the criteria, other factors may be taken into consideration; factors such as additional skills, particular relevant experience, etc. In this situation, it may be decided to offer the post to one candidate with a 'reserve' offer available should the first choice candidate not accept the position.

When the decision has been made, this is communicated to the candidates. In most situations you are notified of the results a few days later, but sometimes you may hear the results the same day.

Other recruitment techniques

Psychometric testing

These are tests that have been devised to assess the personality traits of candidates and match these to the particular post. An increasing number of employers are using these tests to support the selection process. There are many variations on the areas assessed during these tests but they may include a battery of tests for working in teams, handling conflict, work styles, learning styles and management potential. These tests are not usually carried out under strict time limits and there are no right or wrong answers to the questions. The responses give an indication of the strengths and weaknesses in a particular scenario and whether the individual is likely to fit the 'role profile'. They can also be used to ascertain whether the profiles of a team of people will work effectively together, and therefore whether the candidate will be able to 'fit in' with the existing team.

Aptitude tests

It is quite common to require candidates to take aptitude tests, especially in technical areas. They are also considered to be particularly useful where the candidates are not expected to have evidence of aptitude through previous experience. Many computer employers use such tests to identify likely candidates to assess before offering an interview. Aptitude tests will usually be in the form of multiple choice questions taken under strict, and usually challenging, time limits. They will usually include tests of verbal, numerical, analytical and logical reasoning, and are likely to use text-based, number-based and diagrammatical materials. Although practising such tests will not improve your actual ability, familiarity with these types of tests will significantly improve your results.

Skills tasks

It is very common, particularly with IT skills, to require shortlisted candidates to carry out a number of relevant, practical tasks. For example, the candidates may be given a set of data and details of the information to be produced, and required to produce a solution using a spreadsheet package. Those candidates who demonstrate that they can carry out this task satisfactorily will then be interviewed to assess all other aspects of their suitability for the post.

Presentations

Many jobs at this level will require that the successful applicant has not only the skills, knowledge and technical expertise but also that he or she can communicate this effectively. To give the candidates the opportunity to demonstrate this skill, they may be asked to make a presentation about a relevant topic. In an IT environment in particular, this should be done using presentation software and it is extremely important to confirm beforehand as to what software, and version, is available, so that the technology will work on the day. This presentation should be used by you as a way of demonstrating that you possess the relevant knowledge, the IT presentation skills and that you can communicate confidently. Practise your presentation beforehand, ideally to someone who can give you feedback, and make sure that it lasts the required length of time.

Legal and ethical considerations

As a responsible employee and potentially an employer, you need to be aware of the main legal and ethical concerns. These considerations apply at all stages of employment including recruitment, terms and conditions of employment, pensions, training, transfer and promotion opportunities, and dismissal.

Race Relations (Amendment) Act (2000)

The Act defines racial discrimination as discrimination on the grounds of race, colour, nationality or ethnic origins. There are two types of racial discrimination – direct and indirect. Direct discrimination occurs where one person treats another person less favourably than others and where this less favourable treatment arose due to the race, colour, nationality or ethnic origin. Indirect discrimination occurs when the treatment of employees of different racial groups is the same but that such treatment will adversely affect an employee because of his or her race, colour, nationality or ethnic origin.

Equal Pay Act (1970)

This Act was introduced to make it unlawful to offer different pay to men and women where they are doing the same or like work. European Union law has established the principle of equal pay for equal work and the Equal Pay Directive extends this to cover equal pay for work of equal value.

Sex Discrimination Act (1975)

For the purposes of employment, this Act applies to men and women, and also makes it unlawful to discriminate against someone on the grounds of being married. As with race relations, there is both direct and indirect discrimination.

Disability Discrimination Act (1995)

Discrimination occurs when, for any reason related to his or her disability, an employee is treated less favourably than others and this cannot be justified. It also occurs when an employer fails to make a reasonable adjustment to facilitate equal treatment. These reasonable adjustments may include making adjustments to premises, alterations in working hours, giving or arranging training, modifying published materials, modifying procedures for assessment or testing, providing a reader or interpreter, and providing supervision.

What jobs could you consider?

The NVQ at Level 3 prepares you for a very wide range of jobs. The skills and knowledge that you will have acquired will be necessary for many different activities that are part of all kinds of jobs. For many positions, the job will not be specifically an IT position, but will none the less require the level of skills and knowledge that you have acquired at Level 3. For example, the practice administrator in a large doctor's surgery may be required to both use IT at this level and provide support and training for others as part of the job.

Where you are looking to move to a job in a specifically IT environment, there will be many different titles used to describe the jobs you might now be considering and it is useful to examine what these might be and identify both the specific IT skills and the supervisory and support skills required.

Given below are 6 advertisements for jobs that you might consider applying for on completion of your NVQ, depending on your other skills and experience and the option units you have selected. For each of these adverts, make a list of all the IT, training and support skills that you have. Make another list of those that you feel you would need to develop whilst carrying out the job, and a further list of those that you would need to acquire before applying for the post.

College of London
Professional Development Unit
Staff IT Trainer
1 year fixed-term contract
Salary on Scale 6 – £20,670 to
£21,891 p.a.

You will help to develop the IT skills of College Staff using different modes of delivery, for example one-to-one, small or large groups, facilitating on-line learning, demonstration and direct tutoring.

You will have a computing qualification at NVQ3 or equivalent level together with a very good knowledge of Microsoft Office packages and experience of helping people to develop their IT skills, one-to-one and in small groups.

Please telephone for application form and information package.
Tel: 020 7654 3210

Or download the information from **www.col.ac.uk**

Design Co-ordinator

Greeting card publisher requires designer with working knowledge of Graphics applications and exceptional attention to detail, to take responsibility for in-house design (corporate branding, etc.), maintain design database and digital archive and liaise with Production Controller. Involvement in bespoke card designs and e-commerce web content.

Application by CV only

E-mail to Tara@almanac.co.uk

DATABASE OFFICER   12-month contract

Salary: £22,407
Location: London West End

Assisting in the implementation and evaluation of a multi-site pan-London Lotus Notes database, you will play a vital role in the success of the unit.
You will:
- provide database support and produce management reports using a range of software
- present, analyse and interpret IT data
- train non-technical personnel
- have good verbal and written skills
- have interpersonal and team skills
- have an understanding and a commitment to Equal Opportunities
- ideally, have IT work experience in the Public Sector

For information pack call our 24-hour recruitment line on 020 7165 2344 or e-mail personnel@london.org.uk
No CVs please.

HELP DESK ANALYSTS
Customer Support in Health Care Computing
c21K

We have full and part time vacancies for the post of Help Desk Analyst to assist in the support of computer systems in the General Practice market. The successful candidates will join a Customer Support Helpline of 30+ analysts who are responsible for ensuring complete customer satisfaction.

The successful applicants will have at least level 3 computing skills and should be able to demonstrate:

- excellent communication and interpersonal skills
- a keen interest in IT
- experience of NT4, Windows 9x, MS Office applications
- the desire to gain experience of customer support of complex IT and communications systems.

Please apply in writing with CV to: Care Support London SW1 6TF or E-mail to j.finch@care.org.uk

Personal Assistant to Director
Salary £23,000 to £25,000 p.a.

You will provide full secretarial and administrative support to the Director (Development & Partnership).

You will have experience at working as a PA/Secretary. You will need to be numerate and your communication skills, both written and spoken, will be excellent.

You will liaise with both internal and external contacts, making them feel welcome, managing appointments, schedules and meetings arrangements. You will enjoy designing PowerPoint presentations and using IT to maintain records and analyse data. You will be confident and able to work on your own initiative.

Please telephone for an application form and further job details. **Tel: 0161 0987 2345**

Office Manager/ Secretarial Position
Up to £20k

for small, busy PR agency, **London, Victoria.** To run office and provide admin/sec support to PR campaigns and events. Required: excellent MS Office/IT skills, superb organisational and interpersonal skills, **experienced** in managing office computers and providing IT support

E-mail to
maria@yns.co.uk

or fax 020 7123 4567

Curriculum Vitae

Personal Details

Name: Fiona Bennett
Date of birth: 25 January 1975
Address: 15 Priory Road
Manchester
M23 6PV
Telephone: 0161 234 56789
E-mail: f.bennett@abc.def.uk

Profile

A highly motivated and enthusiastic IT support person, with experience working in a range of industries. Wide range of current IT solutions experience in an administrative environment together with a significant IT support role. Proven ability to work on own initiative and as part of a team. Able to motivate and support staff to meet the client's needs and dedicated to maintaining high quality assurance standards.

Career History

Portland Ltd **January 2000 onwards** **IT Admin Support Officer**
Duties include production of IT solutions service throughout the administration department, and the provision of first-line IT support to all administrative staff within the organisation, and specifically for Excel and PowerPoint applications. This includes the identification and provision of training arising from support requests. Also responsible for liaison with technical support staff to minimise down times.

Tickets International **April 1997 – December 1999** **Office Administrator**
Provision of administrative services to finance personnel within the organisation. This included considerable use of Excel and word processing facilities in a demanding environment. All internal correspondence carried out using e-mail and some external electronic links with clients.

Wiley School **June 1995 – March 1997** **Administration Assistant**
Responsible for providing all administrative support to teaching staff within this nursery school. This included all routine and non-routine word processing tasks, use of spreadsheets to maintain petty cash records and production of any display materials requested by staff. Also provided some basic IT training to rest of staff.

C & S Systems **January 1993 – June 1995** **Clerical Assistant**
General clerical duties including routine word processing, filing, telephone and written correspondence with customers.

Skills and Knowledge

I have considerable experience producing working solutions to meet user specifications using a wide range of IT packages including:

- Word 2000
- Excel 2000 with VBA
- PowerPoint 2000
- WordPerfect 6
- Lotus Notes
- Access 2000 with VBA

Education

Hillside School	Sept 1986 – July 1992	6 GCSEs, including Maths and English GNVQ Foundation in Business Studies – Merit
FE College (full time)	Sept 1993 – July 1994	NVQ Level 1 Business Administration
FE College (part time)	Sept 1995 – July 1996	NVQ Level 2 Using Information Technology
FE College (part time)	Sept 2000 – July 2001	NVQ Level 3 Using Information Technology

Training Courses

Various courses including application specific in Word, Excel and Access.
User support within an IT environment (internal training programme)

Interests and Hobbies

I am an enthusiastic amateur historian and also enjoy cycling and walking holidays. I regularly participate in the local community events and am currently setting up a simple network system for three local play groups.

Personal Objectives

Having provided and supported administrative systems for nearly eight years, I have a high level of appreciation of the support needs of this area of work. During the last two years I have increased my expertise in this area, both through my studies for an NVQ Level 3 and also the provision of IT support to administration staff at Portland Ltd. I am ready to move specifically into the provision of IT user support.

References

Mr Stephen Akomeah
Administration Manager
Portland Ltd
54 West End Lane
Manchester
M25 7QS

Ms Patricia Black
Head of Finance
Tickets International
Highland House
Grange Hill
Manchester
M9 2DZ

Fiona Bennett
123 New Road
Didsbury
Manchester
M7 8YA

Mr Francis Evans
Personnel Manager
QA Products
321 Wood Street
Manchester
M4 6TY

26 March 2002

Dear Mr Evans

IT Help Desk Manager

I am writing in response to your advertisement for the above post in the local newspaper last Friday. I enclose a copy of my CV for your consideration.

As you will see from my CV, I am currently working for Portland Ltd as the IT Admin Support Officer. In my present position I am responsible for providing first-line support to administrative staff and organising and presenting training where needs are identified. I work closely with the technical support team to ensure technical issues beyond my remit are escalated for resolution.

During the last two years I have been involved in the development of this service, writing and putting the procedures in place. I have also recently completed an NVQ Level 3 in Using Information Technology, with my role in the organisation contributing to the required portfolio of evidence.

With my proven ability to provide IT support and assistance, together with appropriate training to raise the level of IT skills in the organisation, I feel that I would be able to meet the demands of this post and make a significant contribution to the IT support services of the organisation.

I look forward to hearing from you.

Yours sincerely

Fiona Bennett

CV information sheet

Section 1: personal details	
Name – including title	
Date of birth	
Address	
Telephone number, e-mail address, etc.	
Other – eg NI number	
Section 2: career history	
Employer (1) details	
Start and end date	
Job title	
Salary/grade	
Description	
Employer (2) details	
Start and end date	
Job title	
Salary/grade	
Description	
Employer (3) details	
Start and end date	
Job title	
Salary/grade	
Description	

CV information sheet (continued)

Section 3: relevant skills and knowledge	
Section 4: education and training	
School (from age 11) name and address	
Start and end dates	
Qualifications	
College name and address	
Start and end dates	
Qualifications	
Other courses attended	
Section 5: interests and hobbies	
Section 6: references	
(1)	(2)

NVQ glossary

assessor – person responsible within the NVQ centre for confirming the quality of the evidence produced by the candidates and ensuring that all the requirements of the standards are met

awarding body – the organisation, approved by QCA, which awards the qualification (eg OCR Examinations Board)

competence – ability to carry out the activities specified by the performance criteria to a particular standard

element – each unit is broken down into a number of elements which are described by a set of performance criteria

evidence – the products, statements and other records that demonstrate competence. Organised into a portfolio and assessed against the standards

external verifier – person appointed by the awarding body to ensure the NVQ centre is carrying out assessment to the required national standard

internal verifier – the person within the NVQ centre with responsibility for ensuring that all the assessment decisions made in the centre are consistent and carried out to the national standards. The link person with the awarding body's external verifier

ITNTO (Information Technology National Training Organisation) – the computer industry lead body which sets the occupational standards

NVQ (National Vocational Qualification) – a standard that has been introduced throughout England and Wales specifically for work-based qualifications

performance criteria – the things a candidate must be able to do competently in order to be able to claim the award

QCA (Qualifications and Curriculum Authority) – the organisation that oversees the standards set by the industry lead bodies and approves the qualifications set by the awarding bodies

range statements – these set out the situations and conditions in which the candidate must be able to work and the equipment he or she must be able to use

real work – is where the product or service provided is required and used by a third party. It can be paid or unpaid

real working environment – a working environment which has not been principally created for candidate training or assessment purposes

realistic working environment – an environment which reflects the expectations of industry and commerce by efficiently and effectively using currently acceptable information technology

standards – the set of units defined by the industry lead body that describes the knowledge, skills and level of competence required for the area of work

unit – all NVQs consist of a number of units. A unit is a complete section of knowledge and is the smallest award possible. Most NVQs consist of a number of mandatory units and some optional units

IT glossary

animation – within the context of presentations, this means 'building' each slide one element at a time, as it is required

applications software – enables the computer to be used for a specific purpose, eg payroll, word processing or to play a game

automated routines – activities, often defined within a macro or sub-task, that enable a frequently occurring set of tasks to take place by clicking on an icon, or using a shortcut key

backup – a secure copy of your data files

bitmap – images created in pixels and consisting of blocks of colour

capacity – the size of a data storage or memory device, units include byte, kilobyte, megabyte and gigabyte

cell – the intersection of each row and column; referenced using its *column* letter and *row* number, eg **D4**

chart – a graphical representation of numeric data

configure – to set up the hardware and software to meet the specific user requirements

data – raw facts; input to the system

database – an organised, structured and defined collection of related data

electronic communication – connecting to another electronic system to transmit information

electronic information service – services such as e-mail, online remote databases, intranets and extranets

electronic mail – more usually referred to as e-mail; an electronic communication system that enables the user to send messages and information to a recipient's mail-box and to retrieve messages and information from his or her own mail-box

entity – a collection of attributes, data items or fields; may be related to another entity

extranet –an organisation's web browser-based network that is available to external users such as customers and suppliers

file – almost everything that is created using a computer that needs to be kept is stored in a file

file structure – files are stored in folders or directories on a storage device

form – the part of the DBMS that enables the control of diplay of data on the screen

graphics – the display of information in a pictorial form

hardware – the physical devices

help – the online support supplied with many software packages

image – a graphical form of information

information – data that has been processed and now has meaning

Internet – a network of networks all working under the same *protocol* (set of rules) to communicate worldwide

intranet – a web browser-based network that is only available from within the organisation

licence – an authority to use a piece of software; most software is supplied under some form of licence

links: **dynamic** – links between software applications that are updated when the data is changed

hyper – hot-key links to another element, typically found on web pages and presentations

network – a number of computers and peripherals connected together in order to share resources and access to data, and to provide communication facilities between users

object – a discrete item contained within an application, eg an imported image

operating system – its function is to manage and communicate with the resources of the computer system

peripheral – an item of hardware attached to the main computer

presentation – a sequence of slides of information

removable storage media – data storage devices that enable storage remote from the computer system

relationships – the link between two related sets of data

report – definition of paper-based output in a DBMS. This will let you define the fields to be printed and the order in which they are to be displayed

software – computer programs. Systems software is used to enable the hardware to operate and applications software enables the computer to be used for a specific purpose, eg payroll, word processing or to play a game

sources – where the information originally came from

spreadsheet – a very large, electronic 'piece of paper' which is arranged in rows and columns. It is designed to provide the user with an easy-to-use package, primarily for the manipulation of numerical data

storyboard – a sequence of screen designs, or sketches, that show the layout of each screen, the positioning of the content, the colours and images used and how each screen progresses to the next

systems software – enables the hardware to operate support

table – the database implementation of an entity

updates – changes, often enhancements, to a current piece of software

vector graphics – an image based on a precise mathematical description of the picture, in which each object, a line, a circle, etc., is represented by a mathematical equation of the object itself

Index

A

animation 36, 137
application
form 169
job 164
letter of 170, 181
software 41, 42
archiving procedures 52
arithmetic 82, 97
attribute 109
authority 17, 68
automated formatting 83
automation facilities 130

B

backup procedures 14, 38, 51
best fit 94, 127
bitmap 81, 124, 128
bullets 78, 141

C

calculations 82, 92, 96, 113
CD-ROM 13, 38, 41, 50, 81
cell 79, 82, 92, 93, 96
characteristics 113
chart
bar 101, 137
organisation 68, 137, 157
pie 102–3
colleagues 58, 69–71, 72
columns 77, 78, 92, 94, 117
communication 7, 69, 74, 129,
143–4, 168
copyright 11, 13
csv format 100
curriculum vitae *see* CV
customer base 162
CV 14, 164–69, 179

D

data 3
capture 31
characteristics 113
confidentiality 71
copyright 11
definition 112
dictionary 113
format 94
integrity 4, 108
manipulation 81, 91, 98, 118
output devices 35
processing equipment 34
protection 8–10, 53
security 7
storage 37, 47, 50, 124
structure 109, 112,
type 92, 113
database 81, 84, 108
database management systems
(DBMS) 108, 118
design 14, 22, 61, 71, 75, 93, 111,
115, 125, 134
development 41, 62, 66, 71, 72,
126, 136, 152
directories 47, 52
Disability Discrimination Act 175
disks 37, 41, 47, 49, 52, 62
document 25, 33, 37, 47, 49, 73,
94, 123, 136, 144, 149
documentation 49, 52, 134, 139
DVD 38, 50

E

e-mail 14, 59, 139, 144, 148–51,
166
emergencies 18
entity 109
Equal Pay Act 175

entity relationship diagram (ERD) 110, 112
extranet 152–3

F

facsimile (fax) 144–5
field 109, 110, 112, 113,117, 119, 120
file
    naming conventions 48
    structures 46
filing systems 48–9
first aid 19
folders *see* directories
font 74, 79, 84, 94, 129, 136
footer 77, 94, 118, 136
format 33, 78, 83, 92, 100, 113, 116, 125

G

graphical user interface 32, 151
graphics 35, 36, 40, 81, 101, 123, 124, 128, 137

H

hard copy 85, 103, 130
hardware 30, 38, 51, 67, 143
hazards 16–17
header 77, 94, 118, 136
health & safety 15
    IT–related 21
house styles 74, 94, 115, 116

I

images 128, 137
information 3, 23, 63, 71, 160
input 31, 92, 111, 115, 125
installation 40, 54
Internet 10, 13, 14, 51, 139, 144, 151–2, 162, 164, 169
intranet 139, 152

J

job
    description 163
    interview 171
jobs, in ICT 163–4, 175–8

K

keyboard 17, 25, 31

L

layout 94, 135
legislation 8, 9
    computer misuse 13
    copyright 11
    data protection 8, 62
    health & safety 15
    RIP Act 14, 62
licence, types of 12, 161
line graph 102
links 99, 120, 138, 144
local area network (LAN) 146, 148

M

macro 83, 130
mail merge 84, 120
maintenance 62
margins 76, 77, 94, 127, 145
memory 35, 36
meta data 114
monitor 36
mouse 26, 31, 39, 138

N

network 12, 13, 36, 37, 38, 41, 52, 59, 143, 146, 148, 151–2
    bus 147
    ring 147
    star 146
    topologies 146

O

operating system 41, 46, 48, 51

organisation
  chart 68, 137, 157
  files 48
  structure 68, 157
  work 59, 67
output 3, 6, 35, 41, 85, 92, 103, 111, 116, 125, 127, 130, 134

P

page 13, 36, 61, 74, 75–6, 83, 85, 94, 104, 117, 127, 130, 134, 136, 139, 151, 165
  layout 75, 127
  margins 76, 127
  size 75, 127
paragraph 74, 77, 78, 83
parameters 85, 103, 130
password 7, 13, 51, 54
plotter 37
presentation 61, 77, 84, 94, 115, 116, 133, 165, 174
printer 17, 36, 39, 67, 74, 75, 79, 85, 104, 127, 129, 130, 146
professionalism 66, 71
program 14, 30, 35, 40, 41, 54
project management 60
psychometric testing 173

R

RAM 35, 41
Race Relations Act 175
  recruitment 163, 173–4
relationship 69, 110, 112, 119
report 6, 16, 17, 18, 59, 68, 70, 74, 93, 111, 116, 118, 119, 170
Repetitive Strain Injury (RSI) 25, 31

S

scanner 13, 33, 81
screen, *see* VDU
security 7, 10, 51, 53, 149, 151, 153

sensor 33
Sex Discrimination Act 175
software 11, 12, 22, 30, 33, 38, 40, 46, 51, 53, 54, 59, 60, 67, 72, 143, 146, 148, 151, 153
sort 81, 85, 98, 104, 112, 119, 130
sound 33, 37, 40, 138
specification 1, 30, 35, 74–5, 79, 92, 111, 118, 125, 134, 163, 169, 171, 173
  design 125
  requirements 111
spell check 149
spreadsheet 7, 41, 80, 84, 91, 101, 120, 138
storyboard 126
style 61, 69, 74, 77, 79, 84, 94, 115, 116, 126, 129, 134
system 3, 30, 39, 40, 46, 49, 62, 146

T

table 74, 79, 81, 82, 99, 109, 112, 113, 119, 120, 139
table of contents 83
tabulation 78
testing 5, 6, 20, 23, 42, 54, 173, 174, 175
text 11, 13, 33, 60, 79, 80, 92, 95, 98, 113, 116, 129, 134, 136, 139, 144, 151
  format 79
  manipulation 80

U

user support 60, 64

V

validation 5, 113
VDU 4, 7, 21, 32, 35, 61, 62, 92, 94, 111, 115, 116, 119, 135

verification 4, 115
viruses 51, 151

W

Windows 41, 46, 81
word processing 73, 99, 120, 138
worksheet 98